Tranquility
&
Silence

By

Lori L. Wharton

Proof Positive Editorial Services,
2010 Lulu Author

ISBN 978-1-4196-5744-3

The Second College Edition of *The American Heritage Dictionary* defines pragmatic as: 1. Concerned with cause and effects or with needs and results rather than with ideas or theories, practical.

Acknowledgement

Thank You to each and every one of Danny's co-workers for your unwavering daily support, humor, love, prayers and kindness made even the most difficult days brighter. I wish to extend my heartfelt gratitude to the hospital staff, pharmacists, surgeons, doctors, and nurses who collectively were able to extend a life and ease the suffering. Oncology is a word I never imaged that I would become so familiar with or so terrified of. To Danny's Oncologist Dr. Campos and his entire team of specialists, there are no words to express the love I have for each you! Whether it was a medication change or something more serious, each of you played a vital role in seeing us through. Thank you for your prayers, wisdom, and care. R.N. Vicki, you will always hold a special place in my heart! Thank you for your loving compassionate care, endless support, and for being inspired to help your patients in every way possible; you are remarkable.

Thank you to all of my friends and co-workers for your
un-wavering support, loyalty, and humor. Cindy B. you have given me a lifetime of friendship & love. Joan you never let the miles become distance, you were always there, from my wedding to the funeral and so much more, your humor, love and insight has seen me through the most horrific storms in my life. Blueberry pancakes (yours are the best) and champagne with you any time. Marie you lifted my spirits beyond measure when you would come into to town, I know you were just a phone call away, thank you for all the love! Karen your daily presence was desperately needed, thank you for being my rock, cocktails with you anytime. Doug, thank you for being a fantastic friend and so much more, and for seeing me through the fire and into rain, you are an amazing spirit. Pat & Cindy G. Greg & Sharon, thank you for showing me daily that there are angels, I saw them in each of you. To the families that I have met along this journey that I have been able to help, who in-turn helped me, please know that it has been an amazing blessing and a tremendous source of passion and strength in my life.

Lynelle, thank you for a lifetime of loyalty, love, and friendship! Your amazing gift of music resonates in my soul. Thank you for composing meditation music for me and for your collaboration and creativity during production and recording. Pasta and red wine anytime!

Scott of Proof Positive, you are the absolute best editor! Thank you for keeping my vision while enhancing my life! Your creativity is intoxicating, your friendship and trust irreplaceable. Thank you for bringing out the very best in me on and off camera! Champagne at the ocean anytime!

Dear friends,

I designed this guide book with one intent, to help individuals realize that they can overcome horrendous obstacles in their lives. My husband was diagnosed with liver and colon cancer a few weeks after we married. We faced emotional and physical challenges that I hope most people will never have to experience in a lifetime. Tranquility and Silence gives you many alternatives to empower your spirit, bringing to your life new hope and direction. Join me on a journey into the true meaning of Unconditional Love and share our Passionate Intensity for Life!

Never underestimate the ability within yourself to make a positive difference in your life and in the lives of those around you.

My warmest wishes & blessings to you!

Love,
Lori L.

Danny,

I stood in awe of you, your strength, incredible courage, and passionate spirit that will never leave my soul. Your Love was a gift. Your Life was a phenomenal journey to experience.

Kiss the angels!

Love,

Lori L

CONTENTS

Preface

When God gives you a partner to share your life with, they should be treated as a gift. We are all probably guilty of taking life for granted or not appreciating our family and friends until something drastic happens to serve as a wake-up call (or not). Then you realize just how fragile life can be. How many times in our lives have we heard the following pieces of advice: A high fiber diet reduces your cholesterol? The Surgeon General warns that smoking cause's lung cancer, excessive alcohol consumption causes liver damage. All of our lives we have been guided to realize the consequences of our actions, and since everyone's goal is to live a full and healthy life, we try to abide by these warnings knowing the result will be the wonderful life we've been expecting, right?

I feel that if you are a caring, compassionate, and kind-hearted person, you enrich your emotional wellness. We all learn lessons that attribute to our beliefs and values, further shaping our spirit and expectations for a life filled with love and happiness. The greatest gifts we are blessed with are the ability to love and forgive unconditionally. Friendship is the rarest form of unconditional love. Friendship smoothes the passage to the grave.

We never know what life has in store. It is a treasure chest of riches just waiting to be explored. Who wants to go exploring alone? The pure joy of life is meant to be shared and experienced, otherwise we become stale. It's easy to become skeptical if you allow your faith to waiver (as I have done) when life takes you on an unexpected journey.

All things happen for a reason. We were not put on this earth to endure pain. I am a firm believer that the greater the pain, the greater the rewards. My entire life is a perfect example of that statement.

Murphy's Law was my life. I nicknamed myself "medical mishap." Let me share briefly with you the lessons I have learned regarding faith and persevering. Never give up! Never give in! Now, of course I am not expecting the perfect life, problem free, worry free; however, year after year of horrible incidents and accidents made even me begin to think I was cursed. My whole world was being torn apart; it was one freak accident after another.

I almost lost my hand to cat scratch fever, broken and bruised ribs, fractured pelvic bone, torn knee cartilage, torn ankle cartilage. Do you have any idea what it's like not driving for over eight months? Think about that for a moment: 15 years of casts, traction, surviving being stalked and sexually assaulted, surviving an extremely violent childhood and being diagnosed with Chronic Fatigue Syndrome. In a nutshell, I have overcome horrific episodes of pain and despair in my life. I was definitely ready for my pot of gold at the end of my rainbow!

Now, being the poster child for a medical supply store was not exactly what I had intended on doing with my life. On the upside of that, if you were ever injured at my house you knew you would be well cared for. I had a closet full of canes, crutches, knee braces, and enough ace bandages to play "mummy" with. One cannot endure all of this discomfort and inconvenience without a little help.

I had a first-aid kit for my body, mind, and soul. My prescription for helping myself was not only to survive the storms that came my way, but to always know, feel, and truly believe that the sun always shines. You will find in my survival kit of life classical music, candles, aromatherapy oils, and an abundance of funny movies. I also practice meditation. (not as often as I truly needed). You must be able to relax the mind and calm the body to allow the internal healing process to begin. We undeniably have direct influence on our body, mind and mortality.

If I allowed myself to become hardened, bitter, and ruled by panic and fear, I would be defeating myself. I did not overcome the extreme obstacles and create a nurturing spirit only to destroy it, even when I crumble and completely lose it I never give up! never give in! We create our own destiny and dreams through our values, qualities, and passion for life. If you don't live your life with excitement and exuberance, you gravely hinder your spirit and slowly lose your zest as well as your vitality.

The Gift

~

What is your passion in life? What evokes enthusiasm, excitement or happiness? I have several indulgences; ballet and music make my soul sing. I love different cultures, countries, as well as cuisine. Variety is the spice of life and we are fortunate enough to live in a very flavorful world. Bottom-line—examine all the resources, enjoy life.

One man in particular had no problems in practicing these philosophies to the fullest extreme. As I would soon find out, this man was the cup of life. Charismatic is the word that jumps into my mind when describing Danny. The first time I saw him I was buying pastries (I have a relentless sweet tooth). He was looking quite sharp in his perfectly pressed white attire. I do love a well-groomed man.

I stood in amazement at the cases of yummies; they looked like they should have been in the food version of Vogue. When you have the ability to create something that magnificent, it is a gift. Toss in a huge dose of passion and you get perfection. After being offered a taste, a conversation followed that left me wondering which one was sweeter, the apricot pastry or Danny?

During the weeks ahead, I was always buying pastries, hmm. Imagine that! Danny would share funny stories with me. Now we all know that laughter is the best medicine, and I would have to say Danny wrote the book on humor with his storytelling and antics. Before I knew it we were talking on the phone four to five times a day, then lunches almost everyday. We were becoming close friends; I have to tell you that even having to sleep on ice for months at a time and the agony of physical therapy didn't seem so horrible. The sound of his voice gave me an instant lift.

Within no time at all we were finishing each other's sentences, and spending time apart was becoming less frequent. We definitely had chemistry. The first time he invited me for dinner, I was a nervous wreck. He greeted me with a glass of red wine and escorted me to the living room where it was illuminated with intoxicating candles. The jazz music and incense set the tone for a relaxing evening, it helped calm my nerves. Needless to say dinner was scrumptious. I knew it would be coming from a man who had been in the pastry and bakery industry for his entire life. What I didn't expect was perfection; each plate adorned with creations that looked like art. Fabulous eye candy.

Let's review shall we? Considerate, caring, a side-splitting sense of humor, gifted, creative, and extremely giving. Oh, let's not forget gorgeous . . . dark hair, mustache, sparkling brown eyes and a million-dollar smile. Can you say steal your heart away? He picked up his guitar and sang the most beautiful ballad to me. His voice resonated in my soul.

Love was already in the air with the up-coming wedding of his best friend. After all, it was springtime and being smack dab in the middle of wedding planning central, it was impossible not to explore the possibilities. After a lifetime of gloom, I embraced Danny. He made me soar. He was my gift from god, my treasure chest. My reward, if you will. Never Give Up! Never Give In! God will respond; you must be patient.

As the weeks went whirling by, Danny and I didn't waste a minute of it. One of our closest friends, Douglas, loved to sail, and that was always an adventure. We would go to San Antonio and spend the weekend on the river-walk. I highly recommend it! I also loved visiting his mother; she lives in a small town. He adored his mother; we would stay up until wee hours of the morning telling stories, playing music, and dancing. She would call us super glue and crazy glue, because we were always together. While visiting family and meeting friends, he would take me to the pond and we would feed the ducks, he would play his guitar, and we would lose ourselves in conversation.

Danny and I loved to entertain. All of his friends lived within a stone's throw of one another, and there was always a party. Fajitas on the grill, margaritas by the pitcher, Corona and limes in abundance, and there was always an intense dart game on tap. Danny introduced me to darts, and I loved the game. He taught me to be quite a force, although I never stood a chance against him, Pat, or Doug. Toss Danny into the game and it's all over for me. I pitied the person who stepped in the way of the dart board and a dart being thrown by Danny. And it did happen, not to a person, to our cat. Sylvester was the victim. At warp speed the dart goes flying towards the board, bounces off of the wire around the bull's eye, and harpoons the cat. After the dart hit the cat, it slammed onto the concrete with such force it sparked a little fire. Now, kitty on fire was not a vision that I was looking to make a reality, so with some quick action, all was well and we'll leave it at that. Besides, we are in the middle of planning Pat & Cindy's wedding. Did I mention about 500 quests are attending? Tons of work to do.

Life was definitely good, so when Murphy's Law reared its ugly head again, I was caught by surprise. I wish I could say that this time it was some stupid incident. The end result being a broken rib and fractured pelvic bone. The cause Carelessness! A man in a hurry on the freeway didn't realize my lane of traffic was at a dead stop when he made his lane change. He was driving at top speed. Instant vacation!

Now, the minute Danny found out about what had happened he came to visit me. He brought me flowers and a variety of welcomed distractions—all I needed was him. Danny thought the best place for my recovery should be at his house. He was very concerned about me and wanted to take care of me. During the weeks that followed, Danny was the best medicine. He would carry me to the pool or to the racquetball court to watch him play. Almost daily he would leave flowers on my pillow or write me a sweet note. My every thought was his concern.

During my recuperation, I was able to become further acquainted with Danny's friends. I loved hearing about all of their travels and sharing interests with them. Danny just breezed through life with humor, strength and grace, helping anyone along the way who needed it. It was easy to see why friends loved him.

Now I wish I could I say that I loved being waited on and carried around like Cleopatra, not that I was complaining about being in the arms of such a sensational man, but I was growing tired of being the invalid. As the weeks spilled into months my days were filled with physical therapy, rehabilitation, and endless sessions in the pool and jacuzzi. My nights, on the other hand, were filled with tranquility. We ended our evenings listening to Luther Vandross, wrapped in each other's arms. I could feel his heartbeat penetrate my body. All of my pain and discomfort just melted away.

With Pat & Cindy's wedding just days away, the celebrations had already begun. I wanted what those two had, sheer bliss. This wedding was not one of those that you attended and later said, I'll give them a year or two. This couple was passionately in love! And yes, they did live happily ever after. That is, after overcoming a couple of unexpected episodes. Here it is Labor Day, the hottest day ever recorded, 104. The minute you stepped out of the car you were hit with a wall of sweltering, humid heat. Inside the church was even worse—the air conditioning had broken! Ahhhhhhhh! It was two hours before the ceremony, and it was a full Catholic service. Ironically, the groom is known for his expertise in heating and air conditioning repair. A short while before the ceremony, the A/C was pronounced dead, irreparable in spite of the groom's best attempts.

As the wedding got under way, Cindy was stunningly beautiful in her beaded gown. The music, scriptures, and vows that were exchanged left you breathless. I was catching wedding fever! They blended their beliefs and cultures and created a loving environment for their families and, in the process, taught us all a thing or two about respect and love. Now, I must share with you the most hilarious event of the evening. In assisting the bride and groom with their luggage at the hotel, Danny went inside to get a valet cart. All of a sudden, he came flying down the ramp riding that luggage cart like a bat out of hell, when he hit the curb and became airborne! He flew over the trunk straight into the bushes. Of course laughter erupted for several minutes! He was not hurt.

After the excitement of the wedding, it was time to focus on the holidays. I love a good party, especially when we're doing the hosting. We were most festive!

Danny had warned me about his hectic schedule and my job, which also peaked at the holidays. We knew we wouldn't be seeing much of each other until after the New Year. The only solution was to start celebrating, early and often. First there was the pre-Halloween party, followed by the Thanksgiving party, and finally the Christmas party. All before December First.

Our families loved spending time with us. My mom fell in love with Danny the first time she met him. My sister and her children adored Danny as well. Opportunities for our families to spend time together were rare. Danny's mother, sister, and brother all live out of town, so we made the most of our time. I also used this time to get to know Danny's children. When his daughter would visit over the weekends, I would teach her ballet and all about planets. We would gaze at the stars; I showed her where the Big Dipper was and other highlights in the sky. She was quite captivated. His son would visit on the weekends as well, when we would have pool parties with our friends. He was your typical teenager; we got along very well.

You hear so many horror stories about the kids hating their parent's new "friend." Thank goodness I never had to endure any difficulties of that nature. Christmas is not the time to be fighting with your boyfriend's children. It came as no surprise that we had a wonderful holiday. Even though I barely saw Danny the entire month of December, we made up for it on Christmas Day by showering each other with affection and gifts.

Starting off the New Year, still recovering from my back injuries, was not my idea of a good time. I was facing almost a year of therapy, rehabilitation, and epidurals. Plus those lovely weekly trigger-point injections! 40 in all. Now the idea here is to reduce pain, you tell me, "shots in the back or walking on hot coals," go ahead, take your pick. I can assure you that the end result is the same and the word that pops into my head is NOT relief.

I needed to look no further than to Danny for comfort. With Valentine's Day fast approaching, there was no mistaking our love for each other. The topic of marriage was becoming more frequent. The thought of being able to share my life with him made my heart skip a beat. This man has given me so much joy and peace. I knew his every dream, every thought and emotion. I shared in his passion for life!

Valentine's Day, the day of love! One of my favorite celebrations, mine was off to a beautiful start; something yummy was baking in the oven, the house smelled amazing! Danny gave me a tray full of pastries and candies, a bottle of champagne and hand-crafted chocolate roses. Cupid left his mark on us that day.

Falling in love is fantastic mood food! In the months that followed, we enjoyed concerts, sailing, art fairs, and of course, entertaining. The pool was in full use. For me, love was the ultimate therapy.

With my back injury finally on the road to recovery, I could enjoy life to the fullest. Danny and I were always hearing from people how happy and in love we seemed. We were drunk with happiness and zest for life and each other that left people both envious and exhilarated.

My spirits were soaring high as July Fourth was approaching. I gave a new twist to the meaning of Independence Day. For the first time in several years I was feeling fantastic. I was finally able to start dancing again. I had missed ballet very much. Instead of going to therapy everyday, I could indulge in my passions. So, as you can see, I was feeling very independent, and with my birthday a few days away, let the champagne flow! 25 was looking marvelous!

Life for me was sensational, I was finally able to relax and not feel like the next accident was waiting around the corner. I was completely content. To keep my festive spirit intact was no chore. Danny made it easy, case in point—my birthday. He started my day off with breakfast in bed, champagne, followed by dessert.

We spent the day at the beach; we loved watching the dolphins in the bay. Watching the waves come tumbling on the shoreline, the shimmering sand and the crashing of the waves against the rocks were intoxicating. With dusk approaching, the sky was an amazing site; glowing fiery pinks and reds, with splashes of gold that lit up the horizon.

The sunset was the topic of discussion throughout the rest of the evening—it was spectacular. We ended our evening with the smooth and seductive sounds of Kenny G, red wine, and intimate conversation. When Danny would speak, I would lose my senses. His voice is so gentle. Danny started telling me how much he loved me. He was caressing my face. He said, "I could never imagine my life without you." He took my hands in his, sweetly kissed my lips, and asked me if I would do him the honor of becoming his wife! My heart stopped!

I started trembling as Danny put a sparkling ring on my finger. Tears were streaming down his face as I said Yes! He swept me up and we started dancing around the room. Stunned and overwhelmed by his proposal, I knew my life had come full circle. I kept saying to myself Thank you, God! Thank you for giving me the greatest birthday present I could have ever imagined.

I was on cloud nine! I immediately called my mom; Danny had asked her earlier in the week for her consent. She had been sitting on pins and needles waiting for him to ask me! My sister was ecstatic and quick to start planning. Danny never ceased to amaze me. The following day I wanted to share our engagement news with all of our friends and celebrate. One by one, they all had other plans. I was very disappointed, so to cheer me up Danny took me to the neighborhood pub; I liked the cozy surroundings. The minute we pulled into the parking lot I became suspicious, I began to notice the vehicles belonging to our friends and my family. Danny kept silent as he escorted me inside. The minute we entered, everyone erupted in congratulations and starting singing Happy Birthday to me. I wanted to suspend this moment in time. An enormous party lasted late into the night. Life is GOOD!

Now, as you can imagine, the next few weeks were fueled with jubilation. Electricity was in the air, everyone from co-workers and friends to acquaintances and family were basking in our joy. The energy circuits were on overload as Danny's birthday arrived. In my grand fashion I practically bought out the floral shop, and I had so many balloons I almost couldn't get in the car! It was quite a sight to see as I drove home. Danny made his turning 37 look like 18! He started his special day with some smokin' games of racquetball. His friends have been playing for years together in an almost daily ritual. Ahhh, the quest to kill the little blue ball. Danny was lightning on fire when it came to his favorite game.

Of course the party was a smashing success. I had shopped for months for his present, and I was anxiously waiting for the evening to wind down. As a quiet calm was enveloping the room, I gave Danny my perfectly wrapped package. His face lit up like a Christmas tree as he carefully opened his present. His eyes starting welling up with tears as he opened the black velvet box, revealing a gold-braided chain. As I put it around his neck, I explained to him that there were three braids intertwined, one for our first year, two for our present year, and the third braid for the following year of our marriage. I thanked Danny for completing my life.

Life is turning into one big celebration! My birthday, our engagement, and Danny's birthday were barely behind us. It was Pat & Cindy's first-year anniversary. We all recall their Labor Day wedding, sweltering heat, no A/C. Well, that day was just as scorching! Thank Goodness we were not in formals. The anniversary party topped their wedding reception. It was splendid and, I swear, the entire world was invited.

With all this celebrating going on, it was easy to forget how quickly time was passing and we still hadn't picked our wedding date. I can assure you it won't be on Labor Day! We still had one more wedding to get through; the next month his nephew was getting married. We were both in the wedding party; Danny was to create their wedding cake.

You might as well say that October was over before it started. One advantage to being involved with all this wedding hoopla is that after attending five weddings in six months, I would be well-versed in the planning process. It also gives you a preview of what not to do!

Several days prior to the wedding, I knew Danny would be tied up creating their cake, so it was the perfect opportunity to indulge in my own wedding fantasy. I was excited to try on wedding gowns; I called my friends and off we went to the nearest bridal salon. Walking through the doors felt like stepping into a Fairytale. Gowns of beaded splendor and displays of silks and satin adorned the room. After spending all day trying on gowns, the decision became easy: My mother gave me her antique lace gown. It was magnificent. My sister and I spent the next year adding more than 1,000 pearls, while mother made my extravagant veil.

Several more trips to the Bridal Salon ensued in the days to come. Each time, with friends in tow, we began to create a beautiful ceremony. My sister being my matron of honor, I knew Danny and I would be well taken care of. Tami put the 'T' in talent and already had some fabulous ideas. All Danny and I had to do was to pick a date, which we did; at a carnival the evening we arrived in town for his nephew's wedding. After days of preparation and careful driving skills, the multi-tiered masterpiece reached its final destination. Danny was ready to celebrate and with a carnival in town we couldn't resist. We played every game and had a blast on all of the rides. We had such fun; we were like two kids. We stuffed our faces with popcorn, cotton candy, you name it and we tried it. Danny won prizes for me; he was perfect for the balloon and dart game as well as ring toss. After careful planning and much consideration we decided to get married on May 11 of the following year, in between my Mother's birthday and Mother's day. We always knew we wanted an outside affair, and early in May would give us mild temperatures.

With every wedding that was passing I could feel the excitement building within myself. I was most anxious to marry this man. The following weeks were jam-packed! Wedding planning was at maximum warp speed. We made lists and more lists, and soon we were writing more than we were doing. This had to change, so we decided to attend a bridal convention! My Mother, sister, Danny, and I spent a fantastic day of shopping and planning. This convention had everything your heart desired.

By the time the Holidays arrived, we were feeling most festive. We hosted Thanksgiving. Both of our families and quite a few of friends joined us; we were very fortunate to have had wonderful people in our lives. Our wedding was the prevailing conversation. The invitations were chosen. "On this day I will marry My Best Friend" graced the front, along with a red rose. "The One I Laugh With, Live For, and Love" completed the invitation.

We wanted an elegant dusk ceremony. Black and white strapless gowns, long black gloves, and red roses would complete my attendants. The men had no complaints over our selection. They would be in black tuxedos. Red roses would adorn the lapel. Our vision was taking shape.

Christmas is absolutely my favorite holiday, and being about to be married was the only present I needed. Danny had created an enormous gingerbread house, every gumdrop and lollipop in perfect position. My nieces and nephew loved eating it. The looks on their faces when Danny told them they could eat it were priceless! Needless to say, we had a fantastic holiday season.

Once New Year's Eve passed, the time flew by. Every weekend Tami and I spent doing our list of projects. We all were in high gear. Danny was working on the sketches for our cake. I picked the general layout, and he would design it. He wouldn't let me see the cake until the day of the ceremony. I knew it would be magnificent.

Valentine's Day was exceptionally romantic. We wanted to take a break from the wedding plans for a few days, spending a long weekend at a beautiful hotel by the beach. It was the perfect way to escape. Danny had given me a handmade chocolate heart-shaped box, the scrollwork delicately inscribed with Tijumo ("I love you"). We hated seeing our weekend come to a close. Back to life, back to reality.

By springtime I was ready for the wedding to happen! Emotions were running high, we were rapidly finalizing plans, and on the upside every detail had been taken care of. Doug & Pat were Danny's two best men. Danny loved them both so much, he wanted them by his side. He asked me if they could both stand up for him, and I told him of course! I loved the idea, as did my sister; the thought of her being escorted by two dashing men was just fine with her.

Within days of my own wedding, of course, I was a nervous wreck. My close friends had flown in. Danny's family was also in town. The champagne was flowing, and we celebrated daily. At the rehearsal, my stomach was in knots. It was also my Mother's Birthday. We had a fantastic party; Danny had created her cake in the design of a mini golf course. My Mother has been golfing her entire life; she was thrilled with her cake and admired every detail.

Everyone always says to get plenty of rest the night before the wedding. We were having a 5 p.m. ceremony, so at least we could relax. I knew I would be well taken care of; I was staying at a hotel with my friends. Having known all them for almost a decade, we were having the time of our lives! It was also their duty to get me to the country club on time! I had a restless night, playing the ceremony backwards and forwards a hundred times.

My dreams were about to be realized. It's scary when your dreams come true, not because you're fearful, but rather overwhelmed, because you realize how rare what you are about to be blessed with, love, friendship, truly are precious gifts.

Danny and the groomsmen headed for the country club early that morning. Golf was the sport of the day. While the men were playing golf, I was trying to choke down breakfast with friends. They did their best to get me to eat, but how is that possible with your stomach in your throat! My next task was to paint my nails. Ladies, listen up! Do not attempt this yourself; I was shaking like a leaf! Cindy finally did it for me. Next, it was off to the house to put the finishing touches on my hair and veil. I loved Danny's Sister— she is a very vibrant and spirited woman. We always have such fun together, and she was a great hair-stylist; I wanted her to work her magic for me. Almost an hour later, my veil was in place, and I was beaming from head to toe.

The clock is ticking away. Four hours until the ceremony. The staff was hard at work preparing for our quests; the formal dining room was perfectly set with crystal and china. The aroma of candles filled the room. Mother had everything under control. No disasters or even slip-ups. The winding buffet table was beautifully decorated, the staff did a wonderful job, they were meticulous.

The minute the cake arrived I could hear that the staff was quite pleased. I heard them oohhing and aahhing. The room erupted in applause and cheers as Danny left the room so I could enter. I was awestruck as I gazed at this masterpiece. It looked like Christmas packages wrapped in silver and gold. Five tiers tall, each layer hand-beaded, it took Danny and his staff an entire week to finish. I was moved to tears. I sent Danny a note and a little gift, which was a crystal fish (his favorite type of animal) that I had picked up for him. I told him how much I loved his splendid show of love for me.

One by one, my bridesmaids put the finishing touches on themselves. They had been exercising like crazy so they could fit into their dresses. They all looked stunning! It seemed like a dream. Just as the last-minute touches were being finished, I could hear the music was starting. I was trembling. My heart was pounding.

I peeked through the windows to watch as the ceremony got underway. The moment I heard Theresa's beautiful voice resonating throughout the air, I knew it was time. I began to quiver as I watched our wedding party take their places under the white gazebo. The fawns were roaming by the stream, a magical setting for our celebration. Danny looked regal as he waited patiently for my arrival. I started pacing; my palms were sweating. My thoughts were swept away, flashing back upon my life and the rocky journey that had led me to my destiny.

A wave of calm serenity and tranquil silence washed over me as I walked down the pathway. The brilliant sunshine canvassed the sky providing the perfect atmosphere. I chose the song "Wind Beneath My Wings" for my entrance. To me Danny was the wind beneath my wings; he made my heart soar. When he reached out for my hand, an instant spark ignited an eternal flame in my soul. Our ceremony exemplified love and friendship.

As we finished saying our vows and sealed our love with a kiss, our friends and family erupted in cheers and applause. The sun was beginning to set; the sky was glowing a vivid blend of gold and orange. Just as we began to walk back down the aisle, Danny tugged on my gown and asked me to walk faster. "I'm not feeling well" he stated and his pace quickened. Theresa was singing the song "Just You & I." I could hear it echoing all around us as we made the last turn by the pool out of everyone's sight.

Danny turned white as a sheet and fell against the wall, almost sliding to the ground until I caught him. Our wedding party had just started coming around the corner; they helped us into a private room while the quests were being seated for dinner. Danny sat down for several minutes; he said he felt sick and dizzy. The symptoms seemed to pass very quickly, and he said he felt fine. I was very concerned. He didn't look fine to me, but he insisted that he was.

During the reception you never would have guessed that Danny was not feeling well. We had a fantastic evening of celebration. The champagne was flowing as Doug gave an emotional toast to us; even Danny's eyes were becoming misty as Doug told how very special we were and how much he loved us. Pat followed with his toast. His sense of humor came shining through. Our wedding cake was so breathtaking; I hated to cut into it. Each layer was fresh fruit and cream—it was scrumptious. The cake melted in your mouth and the apricot, blueberries, and strawberries added just the right amount of sweetness that left you craving another piece. Beautiful eye candy.

The reception was in full swing, and everyone was dancing the night away. We continued our celebration into the wee hours of the morning at our hotel. Our friends had a fabulous time, and we had the perfect wedding. The following morning, Danny was complaining of stomach cramps, and he had a slight fever. He insisted on proceeding with the day as planned. We had a champagne brunch with our families to toast Mother's Day, and then it was off to another party at my mom's house to open our gifts. Danny's sense of humor was in perfect form as we sailed through the afternoon in high spirits. By early evening, Danny was still not feeling 100 percent, and we ended our day so that he could rest before we left for our honeymoon.

Once we were home I had him soak in the Jacuzzi, followed by a wonderful massage to help ease the pain. I had the candles burning and the jazz music was playing softly. It was the perfect atmosphere to unwind: The fragrance of the candles and oils filled the air, and a short while later Danny was resting peacefully.

While Danny was resting, I was busy packing for our honeymoon. Danny slept through the night. The following morning he said that he felt fine—his appetite and humor had returned. We figured that he was just exhausted from the excitement of the wedding and the pressure of creating our cake. Danny reassured me that he was fine and had no intention of delaying our trip, so off to the airport we went. A short while later, we were on the plane headed for Paradise. We were very excited to be able to experience such a beautiful island.

We were in the Miami airport when Danny started feeling very sick. He was pale, shaking, his stomach was cramping, and he could not eat. I pleaded with him to call his daughter and former wife, Connie, who were in Orlando so that we could delay our trip, but he flatly refused and an intense argument erupted between us. Rather than argue any longer, against my better judgment, we went on to the Bahamas.

I was glad the flight was only 30 minutes. I could tell that Danny was in agony, and my insides started to quiver with fear. But fear of what, I asked myself. He had always been in perfect health; he was passionate about golf and racquetball. He was a fantastic chef, so he always ate very well. He didn't smoke, so what on earth was wrong? Given all of this, I tried to reassure myself that it had to be some fluke virus. Danny told me that he had always felt fine. Since we had been together everyday for over two years and I never saw anything out of the ordinary regarding his health, I tried to lay my fears to rest. We started descending out of the clouds preparing for landing when the Bahamas rolled into view. It was spectacular. The crystal turquoise waters and the lush white sand beaches looked like heaven. It was stunning, absolutely breathtaking.

When we finally reached our hotel, Danny went straight to bed and I went to the drugstore. By the time I returned, Danny was in extreme pain, his fever was raging, his stomach was cramping, and he was dizzy. I gave him a relaxing massage from head to toe; I had him take some aspirin and Alka Seltzer. I was going out of my mind trying to figure out what was causing him such pain. I had him drink some hot herbal tea to try to soothe his body. A few hours later he was fast asleep.

The next morning there was still no change. He had no appetite, a high fever, and severe stomach cramping. He stayed in bed all day. By the third day there was still no improvement, only now he couldn't go to the bathroom and the pain was increasing at an alarming rate. He refused to let me call a doctor and insisted that it was just the flu—again he stayed in bed all day. I spent my time on our hotel balcony so that I would be close to him. We had a beautiful view of the green gardens, and the smell of fragrant flowers filled the air. The ocean was just steps away; I desperately wanted Danny to feel better so that he could enjoy the heavenly surroundings.

My fears started returning and I could feel my panic increasing as the fifth day arrived and he was still very sick! He had not eaten in almost four days now, and not one of his symptoms had vanished. He was hell-bent on staying in the Bahamas, and after many heated arguments I dropped the topic. I kept giving him aromatherapy massages, aspirin, and herbal tea—it was the best I could do with what was available. I said a special prayer for him, begging God to help him get well.

Day six, Danny was up early with the sun and looking and feeling fantastic! I was stunned and amazed, to say the least. He ordered a huge breakfast, and then he wanted to see the island. We went sight-seeing, snorkeling, dancing, and shopping. He had the energy of a ten-year-old. He was feeling so good that I felt stupid for letting my fears get the best of me. I guessed he must have had the flu after all. The next day he was again up at the crack of dawn and he had made arrangements for us to take a private cruise to a remote island. We had the most romantic day, and at last we felt like newlyweds.

I have no explanation for his sudden recovery, and I certainly was not about to question it. I thanked God for answering my prayer. Our spirits were soaring as we made our way home. We did have one little crisis during our plane flight: The weather was terrible. The rain was pounding against the plane, and the winds were so extreme that it almost sent the plane crashing onto the runway as we landed. I remember Danny looking out the window and he grabbed my hand just as the people behind us starting screaming. I was terrified as I watched the wing swoop down, almost touching the ground. We were all shaken and were so relieved when we finally reached the gate and were escorted off.

My mom and grandma met us at the airport, and we were very happy to see them. They brought 10 rolls of film from the wedding for us to see. We truly had the perfect wedding; there was not one detail we would have changed. Once we were home, friends were there to greet us with a bottle of champagne, the perfect homecoming, Danny was feeling better, so we counted our blessings and had a wonderful evening.

We were home only two days when all of Danny's symptoms returned. I made a doctor's appointment. Of course, Danny did not want to go. I insisted, and after he saw that I was not going to give in this time no matter how much he argued, we went. On the way to the appointment, Danny told me that he was afraid to go to the doctor because he was afraid of what would be found. He told me that he had not been feeling well for several months. I reminded him of his perfect health to help give him reassurance and told him to stop letting his fears get the best of him. We spent about an hour with the doctor who was a primary care physician. He examined Danny from A to Z, and nothing life-threatening was found. Danny was told to change his diet and to rest—the diagnosis was exhaustion and fatigue.

Over the next two weeks he became gravely ill: rapid weight loss, vomiting, high fever, and severe stomach cramping. I took him back to the doctor and we were referred to a specialist. Danny looked very frail; he had lost over 20 pounds in a month. I was panicked beyond words; Danny was terrified about this turn of events.

The week we went to the specialist just happened to be my 26th birthday. I awoke to the smell of a yummy cake baking, and breakfast was on the table. I knew that he was not feeling well, so for him to do this for me was the best present ever! To see him laughing and smiling was wonderful, and we had a terrific breakfast. I hated to leave him, but I was going to be late for work. That evening we went out to dinner, again against my better judgment. Danny insisted that he would be fine. He was wrong. The minute our food arrived, we had to leave. His stomach was cramping and he complained of having a terrible burning sensation in his side. Once we were home we went to the jacuzzi; it helped his pain immensely. Later in the evening he played his guitar and sang to me. It was great therapy for him; his beautiful voice soothed my soul and touched my heart. It was the perfect way to end our day.

The morning we were to go to the specialist I went into the bathroom after Danny and to my horror there was blood everywhere, on the floor and in the toilet. I ran into the bedroom screaming for him, he was lying in bed clutching his side. "Something happened, my side is killing me. I can't move, it feels like I'm on fire," he said. I started to call for an ambulance when Danny stopped me. He flatly refused and told me that he would never speak to me again if I made the call.

He begged me to lie in bed with him until it was time to go to the doctor. The more I pushed, the more he yelled; the bleeding had stopped, so I gave in. I knew he needed to stay calm, so I gave him a massage and had him do some relaxation breathing with me while the soft jazz music was playing. I mentally took him on a journey back to the Bahamas. I had to help him not to be so tense because I knew that his mood would affect the amount of pain that he was in. I tried to call my mom to ask for her help, but the minute Danny heard me on the phone he became enraged—he could be a very stubborn man. Thank goodness his appointment was very soon.

At this point, I began to realize that Danny was a very sick man, and I found myself full of rage. How could something like this be happening to us? I absolutely had no answer. I thought about the conversation that Danny and I had when he first told me that he had not felt well in several months. I had believed that he was letting his fears get the best of him, but now I was beginning to see that I should have probed further into the conversation. I found it extremely difficult to believe that you could get that sick all of a sudden. By now my mind was racing with the severity of his symptoms, and any way I looked at it the outcome did not seem promising. I felt shaken and horrified for what we were about to face.

The time was fast approaching for us to go to the doctor. I wanted answers! No more second-guessing or self-diagnosing. I knew the drive there would be difficult. I could feel in my soul that something life-altering was taking place. While we were driving, Danny told me that he had been reading articles and attempted to research what could be wrong. He said he thought he had colon cancer; he was trembling as he held my hand. My heart sank to the ground as I gasped for air. Danny told me that he knew he was going to die, and he was afraid of going to the doctor because it would confirm what he already knew. Danny kept apologizing to me over and over; he was squeezing my arm and sobbing. It felt like the wind had been knocked out of me, and I had to stop the car to regain my composure. Danny said, "I have every symptom of colon cancer, I can't go to the bathroom or eat, and I have these terrible pains in my side, and I vomit all the time, and this fever won't go away." Danny was shattered as he ran down the list and spoke the words that left me haunted.

Danny was a very wise man, and he told me in depth about the articles he had read several months before. Yes, he did have all of the symptoms of cancer, and with the rapid weight loss it was the only conclusion that one might draw. You don't have to be a rocket scientist to figure out the magnitude of what was happening. Danny was too afraid to go to the doctor several months ago when he should have. I never saw anything that sent up red flags with his health until our wedding day. He was very active playing racquetball and golf. He even ran in a 12-mile marathon, and we hosted endless parties. I pleaded with Danny to wait for the doctor's findings before he threw in the towel. I held him tightly and told him how much I adored him and whatever was found that we would get through it, our love was our greatest strength. It would guide us.

By the time we reached the hospital, I was on the verge of losing it completely. I believed that he had something very serious happening to him, but cancer? Unthinkable! I tried not to let my emotions show. I didn't want to alarm Danny. He was obviously terrified, so I tried to reassure him and be as supportive as possible. I spent the next 45 minutes in the waiting room while the exam was taking place. Each minute seemed like a thousand years. My thoughts were fluctuating back and forth between fear, shock, and anger! Just the thought of Danny having cancer shook the core of my being. I tried to take my own advice: Don't panic! We don't know for sure what is wrong. I tried to stay calm and be patient, but my mind was racing. This wonderful man could be that sick? I know that Danny hates going to the doctor, but to me that was no excuse! The anger was setting in and my thoughts were whirling as I was finally led down the hall to the office. Thank God finally we would get answers. I knew what Danny told me, but in my mind I refused to believe it without confirmation. The unknown was playing terrible tricks with my mind.

I sat down next to Danny; he gave me a kiss and we held hands. The doctor walked in. He had our full attention as he started speaking. "I need you both to prepare yourselves for what I'm about to say." Danny squeezed my hand, his body was tense, and I could hear him breathing. I sat numb and frozen. "Life will never be the same for the two of you after today." I gasped and Danny's eyes shifted to the floor. "You have a very serious progression of a colon disease, and additional testing is being scheduled at the hospital. All I know at this time is the colon must be removed in the very near future, and I also believe that there is something else extremely serious happening to you, Danny." He continued, "You are a very sick man, and I want you to fully understand the magnitude of your condition. Even once the colostomy has taken place, I believe that you are still going to be a very ill man." I could feel the blood drain from my body; Danny and I were holding each other. I was having flashbacks of our beautiful wedding and the words "IN SICKNESS AND IN HEALTH UNTIL DEATH DO US PART" came screaming into my mind in a very haunting way!

The doctor left the room so that we could digest this shocking news. Danny asked me why this was happening to him. "Am I a bad person? I must have done something wrong to deserve this, I haven't been perfect, but I love my children, and I try to help people whenever I can, and I love you, so why? Why, Lori?" " I don't know why this is happening," I replied. I begged him not to lose faith. "We still don't have all of the answers yet, we must wait for the other test results so we know what we are dealing with." I kissed his sweet face and looked him in the eyes when I spoke. "We can handle anything together and right now we know you need to have surgery and we can't speculate on the rest, so let's not lose our heads over what else may be wrong."

The doctor returned to discuss the surgery, but Danny was not interested in hearing anything else, he wanted to go home. We finished our conversation and left with an appointment at the end of the week for the rest of the tests that needed to be done.

Once we were home, we started making phone calls. We knew that Danny's mom and sister would want to be in town for the tests. My mom came over to offer any support that she could. She adored Danny; the two of them were very close. This latest turn of events was very disturbing to her. My sister was very distraught, and she tried her best to encourage me to stay positive. Danny started taking a barrage of medications to ease his pain. I could gauge the enormous pain he was in by the amount of pills that he was taking. I gave him daily massages and we spent the evenings in the jacuzzi to give him further comfort. To me actions always speak louder than words.

We were trying to adjust to the news a little better, and we spent our time unwrapping wedding gifts that we were still receiving. It was the perfect distraction. We had wonderful pictures of our honeymoon and the beautiful wedding video to help take us back to the day when our lives became one. What a glorious ceremony it was; our friends were elated, and the vows that we spoke sanctified our love and commitment to our friendship and unconditional love.

The tests were being done on our two-month anniversary. Reluctantly we all went to the hospital. Danny had three tests done; a colonoscopy was the last test, and it would require sedation. We knew it would be a long day. I was feeling very drained—I was exhausted from all of the emotional anguish that we had been putting ourselves through. At least we would know the full scope of his condition, and I wanted all the facts. Only a few hours into the day I was starting to feel overwhelmed. All I could do was to think about our fabulous wedding—we were so happy and didn't have a care in the world.

Finally the tests were finished by mid-afternoon. Of course, they had no immediate results. We would have to call the doctor's office around 5:00 in the evening. All of the waiting and speculation was not over yet. I wanted to yank every hair out of my head. I wanted answers! Danny was exhausted from the day's events. He was in extreme pain, and he was having trouble walking. Once we were home, Danny took his medication and I gave him a soothing massage. He fell asleep a short while later. He looked so peaceful and calm it was hard for me to believe that there was something so horribly wrong.

With the evening fast approaching, it was time for me to make the call for the results. Danny was in a somber state, and his family was silent as I dialed the number. My hands were trembling and my voice cracked as I asked to speak to the doctor. I was told that the doctor was not in and he would be calling us later. More waiting! Only this time it felt like my world was about to come crashing down around me. By now it was after 8 p.m. and still no news. We figured that we would learn something tomorrow, and Danny went back to bed.

Sitting around the house was gut-wrenching, so a short while later I left to go to the pharmacy to get his prescriptions. I called home and Danny answered. He started screaming at me, "Where are you? Get home," he shouted. His mother took the phone from him and told me to come home right away. I figured that Danny was in pain and he needed his medicine. I knew it was too late for the doctor to call.

I was home in less than ten minutes. I walked in the front door, and Danny's family started to leave the room. I could hear them crying as they walked down the hall into the spare bedroom. I heard the door shut. I looked at Danny. "What's going on?" I asked. Danny started crying, "Come here, Lori, sit down here with me. I'm dying! I'm dying! They called. I have liver and colon cancer." He collapsed in my arms, and I started screaming. "It's very bad, Lori. The doctor told me I maybe have three months to live." We fell to the floor in each other's arms, we were both gasping for air. It felt like a bomb had gone off, and I could see my body parts strewn everywhere. We were both completely overcome by our emotions and his sister and mother had to help us off of the floor. They were shattered; we were all in total hysteria.

Danny kept telling me how sorry he was and how he'd ruined my life. He told me he wanted a divorce! I was stunned that he would say such a thing. He told me that he wanted to spare me from all of the pain. He could hardly say the words that crushed my soul. "I don't want you to have a husband that is dying. You deserve better than that. I'll be dead by Christmas, and what kind of life is that for you?" I told him that there was no way I could ever leave him, and I did not ever want to hear him talk like that again. I kissed his sweet face and told him that we would get through this together. I was devastated; I couldn't comprehend losing this amazing man.

I tried to regain some composure so that I could call my mom. My voice was very shaky; I asked her to come over right away. I tried not to alarm her because she had a long drive to get to our house. She asked me if everything was okay. I said, "No, please hurry," and I started crying. I knew this news would shatter her. When Grandpa died of cancer, it almost destroyed mom. I knew this was going to be just as bad. When she arrived, she had her neighbor with her who is a cancer survivor and a walking miracle. She knew Danny and I very well, and it was a great comfort having her by our side. The words that Danny spoke hit mom like a slow-moving freight train. She was heartbroken. Mother's neighbor stepped in, tried to give us reassurance and focus on what we were about to deal with.

Our conversation was almost non-existent—we did more crying than talking. This is so cruel, I remember thinking as I watched Danny. His spirit was broken and the vibrant zest was gone. I wondered why he had to be told this devastating news over the phone. How could anyone be so heartless? The more I thought about it, the angrier I became.

It was now getting very late, and Danny needed to rest. His family was staying with us, so we said goodbye to my mom and her neighbor and ended that horrible day. As much as I had wanted answers, I was not prepared for this! Danny and I were lying in bed cradling each other. He told me how beautiful I looked on our wedding day and the thoughts he had for our new life together that were now in shambles. He asked me again why this was happening to him. "Why have this incredible wedding only to have it all snatched away? I know that all things happen for a reason, but I can't begin to understand the reasoning for me dying." He started sobbing. "It's so unfair, Lori, I love you so much. I don't want to die."

Just as he finished speaking, there was a loud boom! A spectacular white light came shooting through the window into the bedroom. We were terrified as we sat up in bed and squeezed each other. The bright light turned into a shower of white lights all around us. We suddenly felt very calm and soothed as we sat immersed in the amazing white lights. We were frozen in each other's arms. It was as if a floodlight had been turned on in our bedroom. It lasted for several minutes, and then it disappeared as mysteriously as it had appeared. I ran to the window and there was nothing, just the darkness of the night. I looked at Danny; he was shaken up as he asked me what it was. I replied, "I have no idea, but it was powerful."

Danny said, "It was here in the room with us." I climbed back in bed. Danny and I were stunned by the experience. It was unbelievable and truly remarkable. I had never seen anything like that in my life; the boom that we heard was like an explosion, and we both practically jumped through the ceiling. Danny and I had just witnessed something beyond this realm.

We were so exhausted; we would drift in and out of sleep, knowing that tomorrow would be just as difficult as the day before. Danny was deeply saddened. It was as if someone took a sledgehammer and pounded him with it. How in the world would we actually get through this? Where do you get the strength or desire when you have just been told that you have three months to live? No hope of survival. Not one glimmer of light at the end of the tunnel to guide you. The doctor made it very clear that Danny would not be able to survive this.

I shared the same philosophy that Danny did—all things happen for a reason and people do not enter our lives without a purpose. All we could do was to take things one step at a time. Several hours had passed and it was time to start the day. His mom and sister were destroyed when Danny and I walked into the dining room. My ears had a loud buzzing, and everything was covered in a foggy haze and moving in slow motion. We were both in shock. It was like someone had reached into our bodies and ripped our hearts out.

The very first call I made was to the doctor who phoned Danny with the devastating news. The minute I heard his voice, my anger exploded. "Do you have any idea what you have done? How in the hell can anyone call themselves a doctor when he can call a patient and tell them over the phone he has no chance of living?"

He replied, "With all due respect, you are not the patient, and your husband wanted to know." "Of course he wanted to know," I snapped back. "Not only did you tell him he had three months to live, but there was no reason to see an oncologist because nothing could be done. Basically, you told him to give up. I find your actions cruel and inhumane!"

I tried to calm myself, but it was extremely difficult.

He again apologized and gave me the name of an oncologist. I asked him to put himself in Danny's place. I told him that he took away his hope and gave him no reason to have any faith either. He again apologized and told me to schedule an appointment with the oncologist.

I knew that Danny needed me to be strong, and after a few minutes had passed I was to make the call to the oncologist. It felt like I had just crashed into a mountain. Danny was weeping as I dialed the number. As soon as I heard the receptionist's voice, I started to tremble. I did not want to contribute any more stress to this difficult situation. I knew Danny was watching me, so I took a deep breath and told her that I needed to schedule an appointment for a new patient. I spoke in a strong firm voice, not wanting Danny to know how painful this really was for me. I blew him a kiss and gave him a quick wink. He said, "I love you, too."

While I was on hold, my mind kept reflecting on the bright light that had exploded in our room. The only kind of experience like that I have ever heard of was the angels. Just then the nurse came back on the line and told me to come in that afternoon. I hung up the phone and asked Danny to take a walk with me.

We were sitting by the pool, and Danny said, "I know that I have to go the doctor. I only want you there, no family." I told him that I would be by his side for every step of the way." I had a dream about the light we saw last night," I said.

"What do you think it was?" he asked. I told him that I had read stories and I thought that it was also angels. Danny told me that he had, had many dreams in the past about white lights, and that the angels had been showing him Heaven. He said it didn't make much sense to him until last night. He started weeping in my arms. I told him that there has to be a reason for these things happening to us. I also told him how very sorry I was that he had to endure this, and Danny said that the angels had been sent to help us and it should make him feel better knowing that he had guidance, but at this moment he was not finding comfort in it. I told him to be patient; we had enough to digest without adding to the frustration of what he should feel or what he should be doing. He needed no more added pressure.

We ended our conversation and prepared for the doctor's appointment. I hoped that I was saying all of the right things to give Danny the strength and support he needed. I felt like I was walking on eggshells. He desperately wanted to keep his faith intact. I was very worried about going to the doctor and how Danny would react. My saving grace at that moment was that he wanted me to help him and that he would not be alone.

We arrived at the hospital, and I could see Danny's mood changing drastically. He was very tense and somber as we stepped into the elevator. His palms were sweating and I could hear him breathing. I knew he was terrified. I caressed his cheek and told him that I loved him. He squeezed my hand and told me thank you. We held hands as we approached the floor that we needed. We stepped off the elevator and started walking down the hall. Everyone who passed us just stared at us—compared to everyone else we were the youngest they had seen on this floor. The entire wing was cancer doctors, so there was no question of what you were doing there. It seemed that being young was a sad reminder of just how fragile life can be. Even when you have a whole New World ahead, you never know what tomorrow will bring.

We paused outside the office door; the tears were streaming down Danny's face. "I can't do this; I don't want to die," he said. "I can't leave my daughter or son, and what about you?" I knew that the impact was hitting him full force, so I had him sit down on a bench by the office door. I looked into his eyes as I spoke and held his hands.

"Danny, of course you don't want to die. No one will convince me that there is nothing that can be done." My eyes were welling up as I spoke. "We have to walk through that door so we can get you help. I know you're scared, I am too, but we have to walk through that door and face this together." Danny agreed and within a few minutes I led him into the office. The patients gasped as we entered the room and sat down. Even the receptionist was stunned; she quickly took us back to see the doctor. Seeing all of the cancer patients gave us an immediate dose of reality and the trauma we were in for. It caught us both off guard. We sat frozen in our chairs while we waited for the doctor.

Dr. Campos walked in and introduced himself. He told us about his background. He had a very pleasant personality and a good sense of humor. He was from Peru, and he spoke Spanish. Danny was already feeling more at ease. The light conversation quickly diminished as our attention became focused on Danny's condition. He began, "You both need to be aware that Danny is gravely ill. Danny will need to have radiation treatments right away. Next week you'll start, I will order eight weeks of it. This will help to relieve the internal pain that you have been experiencing. You will have to have monthly chemotherapy, and this will hopefully stop the growth of the tumors in the liver and colon. You will need to have a colostomy to have the colon removed, but not for a while. We must try to stop the cancer from progressing any further before we can operate on the colon." I could feel the room start to spin as he continued. "Danny, you are in the advanced stages of liver cancer. It is the primary tumor mass and is almost completely consumed by the cancer. The cancer in the colon is the secondary tumor mass, and it has almost complete blockage. If it becomes totally blocked, the tumor will burst. You will not be able to survive if that should happen."

The impact of his words left us paralyzed in our chairs. The reality was that his condition was terminal. We saw the results of the tests and it really was horrific. Dr. C, as Danny called him, continued, "Danny, I will do everything in my power to help you, but you must understand that your condition is very severe, and I can't promise you that you will survive this. I wish I could offer a better outlook for you both. I know that you were just married, and I can't imagine how hard this is to listen to. My heart goes out to you. I have to be honest with you, the picture is very bleak.

Danny had just one question. "How long do I have to live?" Dr. Campos was choking back the tears as he put his hands on Danny's. "I wish the news was better, but maybe six months and probably less than that. I really am very sorry, Danny, this is one time when I don't like my profession. Again, Danny, we will do everything possible to see you through this ordeal." He left the room to get a schedule for radiation and Danny and I fell apart in each other's arms.

I told Danny, "You need a miracle, and we will pray for one, every minute of every day until we get one." Danny kissed me and told me how much he loved me. A short while later Dr. Campos returned with the radiation schedule and we left the office.

We were on our way to the car when Danny said, "At least we had the best tans of everyone in the office." He started laughing, as did I. I told him that I had a surprise for him and we weren't going home for awhile. We went down to the beach instead. I had packed a picnic basket for us and brought his guitar along. Danny was very pleased.

We sat on the beach; the waves were lapping at the shoreline as we were lying in each other's arms gazing at the sunset. Just for a moment we were taken back in time to the Bahamas, enjoying our last night in paradise all over again. The sky was on fire with brilliant dazzling colors that reflected off of the ocean—it was beautiful. We kept our conversation light and humorous. If Danny had something that he wanted to talk about, he would. I had no intention of bringing up the diagnosis; that would ruin my purpose for coming here in the first place. This was our escape.

Danny told me how much he loved our wedding, he thought it was spectacular. "I had to choke back the tears when I saw you walking towards me; you were floating and so beautiful. I'm a very lucky man," he recalled. We talked about the parties leading up to the big event and my nerves that almost made me late for my entrance. We joked about Danny's ring not fitting, his fingers swollen from playing golf all day, and my attempt at tossing my bouquet. A sad attempt I might add—I threw it straight up in the air and it crashed into the ceiling and smashed on the floor. Thank goodness the second time was "the charm," and Danny's mother caught it.

It was the perfect way to end this terrible day, and Danny was in much better spirits as we headed for home. We hated leaving such a peaceful setting, but as the song goes, 'Back to life, back to reality.' The following day, Danny asked his mother to come and stay with us for awhile. He wanted to spend as much time together as possible. He was very worried about how she would handle this shattering news once she was alone and since she lived so far away; having her with us was the only solution that made sense. She didn't drive, so her daughter took her home to pack. Danny's diagnosis sent his entire family into a tail-spin, they all had to be tested. Danny's sister was having serious health problems since our wedding, she had not been well at all and didn't want us to know, fearful it would ruin our wedding. She looked radiant at our wedding. I would never have guessed she was so sick. I was very worried for her. I was glad they would be back later in the week. We had only a few days to ourselves. It was a nice relief. We knew that this would be our last time alone for quite awhile, so we did our best to enjoy it.

Trying not to focus on the diagnosis was an impossibility. I was rocked to the core. The best way I can even begin to try to explain is that I was so deeply shaken it affected my hearing, vision, and breathing. I told Danny what was happening to me, and he thought it sounded like post traumatic stress syndrome. I felt like I was living in a tin can, everything echoed, and everywhere I looked all I saw was fog. The buzzing in my ears was so bad he had to shout just to have a conversation with me. I felt like I was in some weird time warp; I would wave my hand in front of my face and a few seconds later I would see it—kind of a delayed reaction, if you will. I could only hope and pray that it would go away soon.

The following days were very difficult. Danny had to tell our friends. He started making the calls to have people over. This was the kind of news that had to be dealt with in person. Of course Pat and Cindy were the first we had to tell. Danny agonized over this daunting task for days. He loved Pat and had no idea where he would find the courage to break the news to them. I told Danny to speak from his heart and the words would follow. There would be no easy way, and the longer he dwelled on it the harder it would be. Danny was so worried about how they would react, it was tearing him apart. From the moment they arrived, he was very withdrawn and somber. I'm sure they could tell that something very serious was happening—it was not like Danny to be so quiet or not want to play racquetball. Danny always jumped at the chance to play with Pat, and I loved watching them play. Cindy loved the game as well and I was envious, since I couldn't play because of my back injury. The question of why they were there was put to rest as Danny started pacing back and forth and began telling them what was wrong. "I've been very sick since the wedding. I went to the doctor and they did some tests." His voice was shaky, and Pat sat speechless. Cindy could see me starting to cry as Danny continued. "I have cancer. It's very bad, seems I may not be around here at Thanksgiving." The flood of emotions that followed lasted several hours. It was the most painful experience we'd had to endure since the diagnosis. Danny was absolutely crushed. It was as if someone had taken a sledgehammer to his heart.

With every phone call we made we shattered our friend's lives. Danny and I were always the ones hosting the parties, everyone loved to come to our place. I held his hand during every phone call he made. He didn't want to tell his former wife and daughter yet, he said he couldn't find the words. I begged him to call; it wasn't like him to be out of touch for so long. He flatly refused! After arguing about it, I decided to shut up. I never wanted to push him, especially now. This task at hand was enormously painful.

The following days were difficult, radiation treatments were beginning. Danny had no idea what to expect, he tried not to let his fear of the unknown dampen his spirits. Keeping his sense of humor intact was vital, and by the end of the first week he was feeling much better. It was not as terrifying as he had anticipated, and the pain was starting to decrease which made his spirits soar. By the second week, Danny was looking forward to his treatments, I was elated that he was breezing right through them. He was feeling so good that it helped him emotionally to better cope with the diagnosis. He was eating well and sleeping better, his energy level was on the rise. By the end of the fourth week, Danny was doing fantastic! He was able to play golf with my mother, and I don't mean he just whacked the ball around a little bit. He shot one of the best rounds he had ever played. Mom was amazed, and being outside in the fresh air with the deer roaming and the sun shining was just the boost he needed to get him through the remainder of his treatments.

With the radiation treatments almost finished, chemotherapy was next, OH GOODY! Grasping the magnitude of his condition was an everyday struggle. I knew what to expect from when my Grandpa had cancer, I remember being alone in the room with him. He was very thin and frail; I sat beside him, holding his hands, pleading with him not to die! I love you, Grandpa, his crystal blue eye's enveloping with tears as he squeezed my hand. He passed away more than 10 years ago, and I still remember every detail like it was yesterday. My Grandpa was a very special man; he had a huge heart, gracious spirit, and a calming nature that people were immediately drawn to. I don't think I ever heard him raise his voice, just laughter. I witnessed the devastation it caused for my Grandma. I had a very clear vision of what might come for Danny. Being in this present situation, my grandparents were very blessed to have had a loving marriage that was just shy of 50 years with happy, healthy children and grandchildren.

Life has a way of pushing you forward whether you want it to or not. Danny was going to be 38 in a few days, so we were planning a party. Danny had very mixed emotions. It was very difficult for him not to look at this as his last birthday. I did my level best to help him realize that in spite of what the doctors had told us, his body did not have an on/off switch. I used the success of the radiation treatments as an example of how great he felt to ease his fears. I did not want his life to become a self-fulfilling prophecy: In many cases a patient has been told they have a short time to live and they give up. There is no way for a doctor to gauge a life expectancy for faith, courage, determination, and an unwavering spirit. I reminded Danny repeatedly that he had all of these qualities and the strength he needed to live each day to the fullest. No doctor could tell him otherwise.

Danny's birthday party was wonderful—all of our friends and family were on hand to help him celebrate in grand fashion. Everyone did their best to lift his spirits by showering him with love. It was an emotional day for all of us; the diagnosis was weighing heavily on our minds. I remember the tributes that were given by our closest friends, and we all found out that the best gifts that were given to Danny didn't come with fancy paper, ribbons, or bows. Pure love was the present of the day. Thankfully all of Danny's family's test results were back and they were fine. Danny's sister was even feeling better, I was elated for her, we had many reasons to celebrate!

With the end of August fast approaching, it was time to check into the hospital for Danny's chemotherapy. I would be staying with Danny; I had no intention of leaving him alone. We came prepared, since Danny would have to be in the hospital for at least seven days, and he would not be able to move at all due to the placement of the chemotherapy lines. I wanted him to be comfortable. I packed his pillows and blankets; I also brought a portable stereo so we could listen to music. I had fragrant candles burning, a few of our wedding pictures by his bedside, and an arsenal of books to help inspire him. Creating a serene atmosphere was vital to aiding in his emotional well-being. Danny's philosophy regarding chemotherapy was very matter-of-fact: Just do it or die.

The third evening we were in the hospital, Danny and I were having a conversation when all of a sudden there was a loud boom, and the same white floating lights we had experienced before were surrounding us once again. They were very bright and calming, exactly like the last time.

We still had no explanation for the mysterious white lights. This time it was not as shocking, but the experience was still overwhelming and fast becoming our topic of daily discussion. The chemo was making Danny ill, and having to lie completely still only aggravated an already horrible ordeal. Every day I would give him massages, and I would help him to meditate. I would have him visualize himself healthy and active; I would lead him on a journey to the Bahamas or the golf course, and when he was feeling really angry or aggressive, I had him focus on racquetball. With the music playing and the candles burning, I tried to create the perfect setting to take his mind off of his situation. Our conversations were hard-hitting at times; he would still question me about getting a divorce and it was frustrating. We were fortunate to have so many people that would come to see us, it was wonderful mood food! There was always a line of people waiting to see Danny. It was a wonderful show of support by our friends and co-workers, just the boost he needed to finish his first week in the hospital.

Danny was very glad to finally be back at home, and his mother was elated to be able to be with her son since she had been unable to see him in the hospital. Danny was frail, and he had no energy or appetite. I would make milkshakes with Ensure and fresh fruit to help increase his appetite, and it helped to ease other foods back into his diet. The medication was much stronger now, and Danny stayed in bed for almost three weeks. He was exhausted.

I was very tired; working everyday and then staying at the hospital was very draining. The insurance and hospital paperwork were piling up; it was taking me two to three hours every night. I found it very complex and time consuming.

Time was flying by as mid-September was upon us, and we were back in the hospital for another round of chemo. I was very concerned about Danny; he was very weak and losing weight rapidly. This stay in the hospital was very hard on him, he was running a high fever, and he was very ill, almost daily. I still gave him daily massages, the candles were burning, and the music was always playing. It gave him comfort when I would read to him. Keeping his spirits up was my biggest challenge. David Letterman (we loved him) and funny movies were the perfect combination. With him having to lie completely still for the duration of his stay was taking its toll. We were anxious to go home.

By the time this month was over, we were both emotionally and physically drained. Danny's anger was on the rise due to his limitations. He stayed in the bedroom almost every day. We were finding out what an enormous strain having company everyday was. Danny and I had no energy for entertaining and visiting with company. We were fatigued.

Halloween was fast approaching, and for us it would mean we would be back in the hospital for round three. Danny had barely recovered from the last time. He had not been out of bed much and was still very weak with a slight appetite. I was very concerned that he was too weak for treatment, so I went to see his doctor. I was quickly learning about Danny's disease. I wanted information about new drugs and if clinical trials underway were producing any type of treatment that might have helped Danny. I armed myself with information; I read cancer newsletters and magazines, anything I could get my hands on to give us some substantial hope. Danny made it very clear that he did not want to become an experiment or, as he called it, a lab rat.

Medication changes were made for Danny; the prescription drug Marinol was added. This is a pill version of Marijuana components. It was to help increase his appetite and calm all the nausea he had been experiencing. I had read hundreds of articles on the subject, and thousands of people who were terminal as well as chronic pain sufferers were experiencing tremendous improvements. I told Danny from day one that I would help him. I focused on every detail of his illness; I wanted him to concentrate on feeling well. It was horrible enough that he was terminal. I saw no reason why he should have to read it everyday on insurance papers and doctor's statements. I sheltered him from that torture. I became his sounding board.

Returning to the hospital for another weekly stay was proving to be very draining. Cindy one of my closest friends owns a quaint gift and bookstore. She has everything imaginable, so when the big box arrived from her shop we knew we were being well thought of and prayed for. She sent Danny a kaleidoscope, music, books, Chinese meditation balls, and a whole host of wonderful goodies! Everything was fabulous; we took the entire box to the hospital. It was the perfect Mood Food. For our wedding gift she had given us a set of wind chimes that sounded like cathedral church bells. The postman had quite a time trying to fit the almost four-foot long box in his little jeep.

By the second day in the hospital, I was wishing that the week would come to a fast close. Danny was taken into surgery for the same procedure that had been done the previous month, placing the chemo line. I was busy getting us settled in—the music was playing, and the fragrance from the candles helped provide a cozy surrounding. I was beginning to worry about Danny. A strange, nervous feeling was sweeping over me. He had been in surgery well over an hour. Last month it hadn't even taken thirty minutes. I started walking down the hall to find a nurse when I felt this sharp, stabbing pain in my thigh! It hurt so much it made me scream, and I had flashes of Danny racing in my mind. I could see him lying on the table in surgery with blood covering his leg. I was in a total state of panic.

When I found the nurse, she told me that a vein had ruptured in his thigh and they were getting the bleeding stopped. I was told to wait patiently and I would be given an update soon. Having this happen was going to upset Danny very much. It was difficult enough trying to keep his spirits up. This was adding insult to injury. He had already been through so much in just a few months, and this being the fourth month of a six-month life expectancy left us teetering on the edge. Now, I'm all for extreme sports and games, but this was one rollercoaster ride we wanted no part of.

I started thinking back to when we first heard his diagnosis of cancer. Danny took out a calendar and pointed to the month of Halloween then flipped to Christmas and in a very soft trembling voice said, "I can't believe this is all of my life I have left." He was sobbing as I yanked the calendar away.

In a very stern voice I replied, "Your spirit and soul do not have an on/off switch! Nor does your body. You cannot put a time limit on Faith, Determination, and Strength". I told Danny that if he believed he would be dead by Christmas, then he would be. If you don't want to fight, then you will die, plain and simple. A self -fulfilling prophecy. After a very lengthy conversation, I handed Danny the calendar and asked him to choose a week or two for us to go to Florida to visit his daughter. That conversation will forever be etched in my mind.

I desperately wanted to spare Danny from this long road ahead. I knew that when he was finally out of surgery he would need a boost, so I called some of our friends to help me. Pretty soon the room was buzzing with laughter. Danny was very happy to see Doug. It was the perfect way for him to forget about the mishap during surgery. Of course, the topics of conversation were about racquetball and golf the many weekends they spent helping Danny perfect his game. Since racquetball was out of the question, he found a new love in golf: It rejuvenated his spirit.

I would give them their privacy when they came to visit. I wanted Danny to be able to be comfortable talking about his cancer openly and listening to what his friend's concerns were. I used the time away from him to make phone calls or to slip away with friends for an escape, even though I felt extremely guilty. Danny had been pressing very hard on me to get out and live life rather than be at the hospital so much. There was an enormous amount of guilt on both our parts. I found that you can try to do everything in your power to have a few days that aren't consumed by the illness, but your mind keeps a vivid account.

As the week wore on, co-workers and friends were flocking to the hospital in grand affair, each one armed with flowers or games and always food. It helped Danny so much to see his staff; he missed working very much. With this hospital visit turning into a three-week stay, I had all of my resources in full swing on the morale committee.

Danny was running a high fever, and his pain was increasing. Each day began the way it ended, with massages, music, and quiet meditations. I was quickly learning how much it was helping him. Danny's pain wasn't as intense, and the herbs, teas, and oils that I used definitely helped him to relax and sleep better. It also gave us both a chance to release the tensions of the day, to erase the pain. This time was very special to us. I would start with a peppermint lotion foot massage to stimulate his circulation, and immediately Danny could feel the pain subsiding. He would sip hot herbal tea while I would finish the rest of his body massage. I used warm herbal massage oils on his shoulders, chest, and back to help with his breathing and circulation. You can't have chemotherapy pumped into your body and then just lay there. Your body will become like a sponge, so a massage is the perfect way to keep the blood flowing and the heart pumping oxygen into the bloodstream. The liver being the detoxification organ and Danny having liver cancer, it was very important to keep the circulation going.

After a long stay in the hospital, we just wanted to collapse at home, and each weekend Danny's family would come to see him. Danny liked to see them, but it was very difficult for me because I spoke no Spanish and most of them didn't speak English. It made me feel like an outsider in our home. Tensions at our house had already been running high, almost every night there would be a flaring argument between them. Their sharp-tongued comments left a stinging impression in my mind. Danny and I relied heavily on one very close friend for guidance and suggestions. I wanted Danny and his family to be at peace with each other. It was always dueling Bibles and the battle over religion and healing. Danny didn't believe in certain religious practices as his family did, and it sparked an all-out war between them. He put all of his unwavering faith in Gods hands completely. Sadly, they made it very clear to us that I was the reason that Danny was dying. I was told that if I would take him to church he would be just fine. Danny wasn't able to attend services because of his health, but that didn't stop us from praying daily; you don't have to be in church for God to hear you! God looks beyond your actions, he knows your heart and he does answer prayers.

Danny was very conflicted over the religious arguments. Week after week of the fighting wore me down. I dreaded each day because nothing I did or said improved the situation, and it made me very angry and left me full of distain.

My home was not so happy; all I wanted was for all of us to help Danny in the way that he wanted.

Whether your religion is Danny's belief or not, cancer is very horrific, you can't have fighting on a daily basis, and the stress was unbearable. I couldn't sleep or eat much. I was suffocating in their constant turmoil. It was very painful to watch our family unravel. I know how shocking the diagnosis had been on them, anger and frustration had become a sad realization. I desperately wanted the fighting to stop. I wanted for each of us to have our happy lives back! We were all put in such a terrible position. His mother would pray non-stop with her rosary. I watched her, hoping that the prayers were being heard and answered. I wanted the same miracle they did, for complete healing! We just had very different ways of speaking to God!

With so many hurdles ahead of us, we had to focus on ourselves and take this time to relax and nurture our spirits. He just wanted to be alone and made that very clear to all of us. It was a bitter pill to swallow. Danny asked his family to leave, I was very worried about him becoming increasingly isolated. Faith, healing, and love are supposed to bring you together, right?

Danny and I were realists. We knew he needed a miracle to survive. We prepared for the worst, prayed daily for the best, and planned for the future. Each day that passed was one more we were grateful to have, and we slowly put the pieces back together. He was still mumbling about divorce and started laying out a plan for me. At this point, I just wanted to be able to have our friends over so that we could hear music and laughter once again. I missed my friends—I took full advantage of having our home to ourselves. Danny and Doug couldn't resist a light jam session. In no time I felt like I was at a concert. Danny would lose himself in his music, and the songs he wrote made his spirits soar. It was a daily grind to stay motivated, but at least we were trying to learn to live with cancer and making the necessary adjustments to do so, as were our close friends.

Now with Thanksgiving almost here, I had one major concern: Danny still had not told his daughter. He said he couldn't find the words. The more I pushed the issue, the more Danny flatly refused. I knew it would only be a matter of time before Connie called us. It wasn't like Danny not to talk to them in so long. His closest friends even tried to convince him, but to no avail. It was tearing Danny apart inside; he had terrible nightmares.

That Thanksgiving we truly had reason to be very thankful and grateful to God for giving Danny the holiday. If you had to judge a person's health by their attitude, you would have said that Danny would live to be 100. Our family's were together, there was no tension. It was wonderful. Inside the frail body was a sharp and funny brilliant mind, and his compassionate spirit was undeniable. He had one regret: not going to the doctor sooner. We did not talk much about the conversation we'd had months ago when he first told me he knew he had cancer. Slowly I started hearing from his co-workers that he had been quite sick at work, and they had expressed concern about his health months before we were married. I was not amused!

The obvious question at this point is, if I had known he was dying would I still have married him? Without a moment's hesitation, my answer is YES! Do I wish I had known before we were married? YES!!! I'm the kind of person who likes to have all the facts. It would have answered many questions. Even though I never saw anything catastrophically wrong, there were subtle hints. During the last few months before the wedding, Danny became very short-tempered on a few occasions, and his affection seemed to almost disappear. I tried to ask him about it and he always told me not to worry, but I did. His lack of attention left me alone and upset more than a few nights. He asked me to please be patient and blamed his temper and distance from me on stress. His actions for that brief time period were completely uncharacteristic. I accepted his answers and believed in him.

Danny can be a very stubborn man. Case in point: his daughter. My one major concern manifested into a harsh reality. Connie, his former wife, called Danny's workplace over the Thanksgiving holiday. She was told by a complete stranger that Danny had cancer, would not be returning to work, and maybe had a couple of months to live! She immediately called the house. I answered the phone. She was devastated!

The minute I heard her voice I started to tremble; I could hardly speak. I handed Danny the phone, and he had a very long conversation with her. I was crushed. Having to listen to the pain in his voice as he spoke really crushed me.. I knew Danny would need all the support he could get, so while he was on the phone I was busy packing us a picnic basket for an afternoon at the beach. I wanted Danny to be in a soothing surrounding to help calm his spirit. He told me they wanted to come and visit us very soon. I loved the idea! Danny was very excited about seeing them and he felt an enormous amount of guilt for not calling.

Over the next few weeks, she and I spoke to each other almost on a daily basis. I wanted her to be involved with Danny's care, and I kept her up to date on his treatments. Our conversations were very candid; she knew exactly what he was facing. I knew that Danny loved her very much, and even though their marriage of 10 years had come to a close, he cared about her deeply. I welcomed her advice and the many hours a week that I spent on the phone with her were the bright spots in my day. We became very close friends, and I loved her very much. We all had the same goal: To shower Danny with support and help give him the strength and courage to continue his fight!

Being in the hospital during Christmas facing another round of chemotherapy was no picnic. Our saving grace was that he would be able to have the portable catheter placed in his chest for his treatment instead of his thigh. This gave Danny the freedom to walk around and be able to sit up. He was feeling more like himself and less dependent on others. No holiday would be complete without friends, and once again they made Danny's spirit soar!

By Christmas Day we were back home, and Danny was feeling very good. I planned a special surprise for him. I knew that Danny's family would want to see him. I hated the tension between us. I didn't want the past events to hinder the future. I truly believed that in time they would know that Danny was the light of my life, and his every need was fulfilled. Danny was very happy when he learned of my plans. We stopped by my mom's house for a brief visit; she was delighted to see us. Danny missed her very much.

By mid-morning we were on our way out of town. We listened to Christmas music and sang songs during our two-and- a-half-hour drive. There was a chill in the air and the sun was shinning; it was beautiful. The perfect way to celebrate the day! For the first time in his life, Danny was not caught up in the whirlwind of the Christmas season and having to work. It was a very special time, and we savored every moment of our tranquility. We were in high spirits and feeling very festive when we arrived at his sister's house.

Danny's mother and sister cried tears of joy when they saw him. They thanked me for bringing him, and for the first time in months I felt like a part of his family. His sister and I had wonderful conversations; I explained to her what it was like for Danny having the tension in his family. I wanted her to understand Danny's wishes and even though I didn't agree with some of his decisions, I had to support him. She knew that her brother could be very stubborn and that this was about Danny's life and how he chose to live it. She was also aware that it was very difficult for me to abide by his wishes. Danny had been very hard on me when it came to his choices. It was either his way or the highway, and in many situations it was easier to give in than to have a heated argument. Life is far too precious to waste!

After spending a wonderful afternoon with his family, it was time for us to leave. I invited them to come and visit us when his daughter arrived. They were elated! Danny asked me to take him somewhere on our drive home. He was being very mysterious. I followed his directions and noticed he was becoming very quiet. As I made the last turn to drive up a hill, he gently held my hand, asked me to be strong, and to please not cry. I was very puzzled until I saw where he was leading me. The CEMETERY! Danny told me he needed my help. My mind was racing, and my heart was pounding so hard I knew it would burst. I drove into the cemetery, and Danny told me where to stop. We stepped out of the car, and Danny pointed to a burial plot. He said, "This is where I want you to bury me, next to my Grandfather."

I was speechless; tears were streaming down my face. Danny gave me a hug and said, "You know this could happen and I want to make it as easy for you as I can." He begged me to be strong and told me that funerals are for the living, that he would be in Heaven with God, watching over me just as the angels that always came to visit us. I promised Danny that I would make the rest of the arrangements. The crisp cool air was sweeping over the hill stinging the tears on my face. Our wedding vows were racing in our thoughts.

I glanced around at the grave markers and I saw the headstone of a little boy. I remember feeling very blessed that Danny and I were given this time together. We had a very long conversation about how very different this Christmas was than the last. On this day there was not the excitement of opening his presents, acting like a child at 5 a.m. enjoying his new toy. I will never forget the fun and bliss we shared on that day as we listened to the soundtrack from the movie The Fabulous Baker Boys. We danced and sang until mid-day. James Brown and The Eagles provided the instant concerts for us, and it was marvelous!

We had a very quiet New Years Eve. Each holiday that passed brought us closer to the reality that we may not have another one to share with each other. We had been so very blessed to have the time we had been given, but with this New Year we didn't make silly resolutions that are rarely kept. We wanted a miracle, and we hoped and prayed that we would be able to spend many more years to come drinking champagne, hosting great parties and watching Dick Clark.

The following week, his daughter and Connie were finally here. Danny was very nervous. I tried to help through this difficult time: I gave them privacy. I wanted them to spend as much time alone as possible. We all wanted the same thing: for Danny to know how much we loved him and were committed to helping him. We really were able to help Danny relax and enjoy the time together. We stayed up late, talked, and laughed about the past and the irony of it all. Most people would find it very strange that the former wife and the new wife became so close, but to Connie and me it was perfectly normal.

When the few days had come to an end, there were many tears and heavy hearts, but we were all so thankful that we were given this time together. Danny and I were planning a trip to Florida in the spring to visit them. Through it all we never stopped planning ahead, and I know that this is one reason why Danny was able to handle his diagnosis as well as he did. We never tried to dwell on what the doctors were telling us. We accepted it, but so far they were wrong. Danny and I loved life too much to let them hinder our future.

Danny was in much better spirits after seeing his daughter, and he was in a good mood as we checked back into the hospital. Here we were again armed with books, music, and candles. His body was weak, and the pain was increasing. Meditation and massage were still part of his daily routine. It helped him with the frustration and anxiety. I was happy to be able to help him. Only a few days into the treatment, Danny became very sick. He had a very high fever and was vomiting. He would have to stay in the hospital for much longer, and we were told that he would have to have surgery. A colostomy needed to be performed, and given his condition, the surgery looked fatal to me.

Danny's dreams were very vivid, and each morning he would tell me about Heaven and how the angels would show him things. He called them visitors, and he told me of several times that he would see me when I was alone. He recalled when the vein burst in his thigh and the sharp pains that I had in my thigh at that exact moment. He also shared with me many more experiences, like when he saw me praying for him when I was alone. He told me that we were connected because of our love for one another.

The week of the surgery just happened to be during Valentine's Day. I knew the surgery would be very difficult for Danny to survive. The doctors told me that he probably wouldn't. I stayed focused on my goal of helping him through it. I brought the book *Love, Medicine, and Miracles* to read to him, and it helped give him comfort and strength. It is a wonderful book by Dr. Bernie Seigel about cancer patients and their inspiring stories of survival and defying all obstacles. I read the book from cover to cover many times to Danny, and it gave him the reassurance and courage that he needed. We had been told many times before that he was not going to survive. We knew that we had to put our faith and trust in God to see us through.

The morning of the surgery, the doctors met with me and told me that I needed to prepare myself for the worst, that Danny was probably going to die. I asked them not to tell him, that I needed some time alone with him before they took him into surgery. My mind was reeling, and I pulled a chair over to his bed and started caressing his face. I could not shed any tears: It was crucial that Danny see me strong and inspiring. Danny smiled at me and told me that he didn't think he would make it. He handed me his wedding ring. "I love you, Lori. I think my body is giving in, and if I die on that table you have to be strong." The tears were gently falling down his cheeks.

My voice was cracking as I spoke, "When you are in surgery I want you to think of our love, and you know that I am with you. I want you to feel my presence in your soul and in your mind. You will know that you are not alone, and when you get scared just know that the angels are with you and they will guide you back to me".

Just as I finished my sentence, the doctors walked in and it was time. I held Danny's hand the entire way as he was wheeled into surgery, then I leaned over him, put my hand on his heart, and told him that I would be right here waiting to put his wedding ring back on his finger. I kissed him on the lips and said, "You be strong, Danny. I love you with all of my heart. Don't you give up, because I never will." I could only watch as he was wheeled the rest of the way into surgery and I was shouting, "I love you, Danny! I love you! I love you."

I immediately ran back to the room and locked myself in the bathroom: I shut the lights out and sank to floor. It was a tidal wave of emotional anguish. I started praying: I begged God to bring him back to me as I clutched his wedding ring. Suddenly, there was a knock on the door; it was a nurse telling me to go to the surgery waiting area. I didn't realize that almost an hour had gone by, and I could barely stand. I took a deep breath, and as I was reaching for the knob, I heard a very faint voice telling me to be calm and patient. It was soothing, and I felt a wave of serenity wash over me. The loud buzzing and foggy haze I had experienced since the day of the diagnosis had vanished. I had a presence of warmth and peace on my shoulders. I could feel Danny's heartbeat, and I started having flashes of him during surgery. With my mind I placed myself on that table, lying inside him, filling his soul with love and comforting thoughts.

Our family and friends were in the waiting room, and I spent the next two hours outside with my sister and a few of my closest friends. I focused completely on Danny. I spoke very little and went completely inside myself praying that Danny would feel peace and comfort. I never shifted my focus, and before I knew it the surgeon came looking for me, only it was too soon. The surgery was due to take about three hours and it had only been two, I could feel myself start to crumble. My sister was shaking me back and forth telling me to pull it together. I kept saying, "It's too soon, it's too soon." She had to practically slap me back into reality. She said, "Get in there and find out what's going on." She opened the door and pushed me inside. Again I felt this amazing, calming presence on my shoulders as I walked over to the surgeon.

I tried not to panic. "Remain calm," I kept telling myself. I braced myself, and I felt the blood draining from my body as he spoke. "Danny is asking for you, he is in recovery." I started jumping up and down and screaming with elation. I threw my arms around the surgeon, gave him a kiss on the cheek, and shouted, "He made it! He made it!" The waiting room erupted with cheers and clapping. I was crying tears of sheer joy! I immediately ran back to his room, locked myself in the bathroom, sank to floor, and thanked God and the angels for watching over him. I was so grateful I couldn't stop sobbing. I returned to the surgery wing where the family was, and we all shared the incredible news. Then I went to the recovery area, but the nurses would not let me be with Danny. I could hear him calling for me, and I begged them to let me see him. They were very sharp with me and told me no, absolutely not. I pleaded with them as they led me back into the hallway.

I started crying hysterically. "You don't understand. Please, I have to give him his wedding ring." I opened my hand and showed it to them. I begged them, but it was no use. I had an indention in my hand where I had been clutching it so tightly. I sat on the floor right outside the doors. I could hear Danny calling for me, and it was torture, sheer torture. A few moments later, Dr. Campos came by and asked me what was wrong. "Danny is doing fine. Why are you upset?" He helped me up off the floor and I started crying in his arms. I told him that the nurses wouldn't let me be with him, that they gave me a lecture and escorted me out, that I could hear him calling for me. He said, "Come with me." He led me inside and told the nurses to give me some sterile scrubs. He was very stern with them as he told them not to keep us apart. "These two are special." He flashed me a smile and left so I could be with Danny. I thanked him as he walked away.

I was led to Danny's bed, and he said, "Where have you been? I've been calling for you!" I took his hand as I kissed his face. "I heard you calling my name. I'm right here where I've always been, with you." Danny held out his left hand and asked for his ring. Tears were streaming down my face as I placed the ring on his finger.

"I came back just for you," he said. "I tried to leave, but the angels brought me back, I saw you praying for me in the bathroom. Why were you crying so much? I told you to be strong. I'll always be with you. I love you." "I love you too, Danny." I leaned over and gave him a kiss. Just as I did, the entire room was aglow with dancing lights, only this time they were pale pink, gold, and blue colors, moving very slowly all around us. It was incredible.

Danny said, "It's them. They came to see us again." He smiled and said, "They showed me what it will be like for me up there. I know that I will die, but you can't be sad when I have to travel." He squeezed my hand and told me I had to be stronger or he couldn't leave. "I'm not leaving for awhile," he said in a calm, soft voice. "Everything will be all right, and when the time comes I will help you and so will they." He pointed to the floating lights. "They will guide you. You can do this, and with my help you can go on with your life. You must move on because I will be healthy and I won't have any more pain. You need to be happy for me when the time comes." I began to cry, and Danny wiped my tears away.

Danny told me to go back to the room and wait for him there. He gave me a kiss; the bright glowing lights disappeared, and he fell asleep. I sat next to him and held his hand until the nurse told me to leave. I asked her if she noticed anything out of the ordinary during my visit, and she said no. The lights were so bright, I just knew that someone else had to have seen them. As I was walking out, she made a comment about the clock hanging above Danny's bed; it had stopped at the exact time that the lights appeared. She told me that it had been working fine all day until now. I told her I had not been paying attention to it, but it was working when I first arrived. I asked for the correct time and she told me that I had been visiting for over 45 minutes. Then she became angry with me for staying so long. I was surprised at what time it was because it seemed like only a few minutes. It was as if time had stood still for us.

I went to the waiting room where our families were. They told me that I had been with Danny for almost an hour and that they were getting worried. I reassured them that Danny was fine, and he would be back in his room soon and to wait for him there. I left to go upstairs to see his doctor. I wanted to thank him for letting me see Danny. I waited in his office. I couldn't help but think about the experience that I just had and the conversation with Danny. There was no doubt in my mind that the bright lights were the angels, and I felt very blessed by God that I was allowed to share such amazing, life-enriching circumstances. What we were being shown was far greater than the terminal diagnosis we were given.

The power of love and prayer was our driving force. Together we were truly united, a bond that not even death would separate. I felt a new-found strength and rejuvenation that I had not experienced since our wedding day. I was swept away in deep thought as his doctor entered the room.

Dr. Campos asked me how Danny was doing. I told him that he was in good spirits and resting when I left. I did not elaborate on any other details. He asked me where my strength and courage came from; he called me a rock! I laughed and said, "I don't feel like a rock". Our conversation turned to the situation at hand. I knew very little about the colostomy. We had a very frank discussion about the physical limitations and the adjustments that would need to be made. Even though his pain was greatly reduced, the cancer was progressively growing. He would need to have full-time care and his activities would probably be non-existent as the cancer progressed. The medication for his pain would be stepped up.

We finished our discussion and I returned to the room. It was scary for me to see Danny hooked up to all of those machines. I would not be able to stay with him this time because there was a patient assigned to the other bed. How very strange we knew him—he was our pharmacist. I was relieved to have someone who had taken such good care of us in the next bed. From day one, he had been a godsend to me. I saw him on a daily basis. He always took extra time with me to fully explain all of Danny's medication, and he researched drugs that might be more effective. He was a caring and compassionate man. God gave me earthly angels as well! I knew that Danny would be in good hands when I was not there.

I was later introduced to the hospital pharmacist who prepared Danny's chemotherapy. He gave me insight into more effective treatments for pain, which proved to be vital in the days and weeks to come. It was a great comfort to have people close to me that were caring and compassionate. I leaned on Doug for extra doses of support. Jim and Cindy tried to help us any way they could, as did Chris and Delores; we needed their laughter and love. This reality was such a strain on friendships. You don't know how to act or react, it wasn't singing around the bar and fun all the time anymore, and that can twist anyone's mind and spirit inside and out!

Being away from Danny was very painful for me. Even though I knew that he was in good hands, I was glad to be home after a few weeks at the hospital. I had some of Danny's family staying at the house, I desperately wanted to be alone.

I called the hospital many times during the night to check on Danny, and even though he was doing fine I did not sleep much. I was completely exhausted, but my mind was in overdrive, concentrating on what the future had in store for us and the experiences that would come with it. I do believe in the angels. They came to visit us so many times, it was impossible not to. Even though I knew we were not alone, God guiding our lives, it was still hard to prepare to let go if that truly was our fate.

Only two days had passed when his doctor asked to see me. I knew that something serious was happening because he always knew where to find me, and it never had been this formal. Danny was in good spirits and he did not seem to be having any problems, so I was a little puzzled. Once at his office, he did not mince words when we spoke. He informed me that even though the surgery was a complete success, the liver was not doing well at all and that Danny would probably not live much longer. The liver was no longer responding to the chemotherapy, and the tumors were growing at an alarming rate. Suddenly my entire world was blown apart. He told me to get our affairs in order and prepare myself for what was coming. He told me how deeply sorry he was, tears were streaming down my face, and the room started spinning. He told me that the next few weeks were crucial, but I needed to be emotionally strong, and that it would be best if I didn't tell him this latest news.

I decided at that moment that I needed to leave my job, so I went to work and resigned. It was for the best, they had been very understanding regarding my situation and I could not have asked for a better company to work for, but they needed an employee who they could rely on, and I was not able to be that person any longer. It was a very emotional day for all of us; the ladies I worked with were very supportive and loving. Chris immediately put Danny on her church's prayer list. Pam and Terri always greeted me with awesome wit, love, great dinners, and even better lunches. They saved me from completely losing my marbles! It was very hard to say good-bye; I would miss them all so much. They made it possible for me to function while I was at work and I will always be grateful to each and every one of them for their support. It was very difficult to give up something that I loved so much. But I had no choice, Danny needed me.

I had my mother come to the hospital that evening so that I could tell her the crushing news about Danny. We went to the nursery; I loved spending time up there with all of the little babies and proud parents. I would go up there late at night when it was quiet and I would watch the babies, it seemed to re-affirm the joy and fragility of life. Mom and I had a lengthy conversation, and after many tears we returned to Danny's room. We checked our emotions at the door; I had one rule that I never wavered from: NO TEARS ALLOWED. Danny needed smiles only in his environment.

I was relieved not to have the worry of leaving Danny alone. Even though I loved my job and the people I worked with, I needed to be with him and I had wanted to since day one of the diagnosis. Being torn between work and the hospital was the greatest anxiety I had ever experienced. I felt very blessed to accommodate his every wish.

Adjusting to the colostomy was a huge ordeal for us. He needed my support and strength like never before. A nurse was assigned to help me understand the care and maintenance involved. This would be the first time that I had seen the results of the surgery. Now, I'll tell you right off the bat that I fell apart. I have never been a strong person when it comes to medical procedures, and it was only by the grace of God and by the skin of my teeth that I had done so well this far. I became physically ill when I saw the colostomy and how it affected his body. I couldn't even be in the same room while the nurse was showing Danny the necessary steps to care for it. Each time I tried so hard to control myself, but to no avail, I always ended up in the bathroom with my head in the toilet.

Everything that I had done for him with the massages, music, books I read to him, and my constant faith and love could not get me past this obstacle. Danny started pulling away from me, and over the next few weeks he wouldn't let me near him. He barely spoke to me. I tried so hard not to get sick and to be supportive, but I was finding out that just because I wanted to help him did not mean I would always be able to. This was proving to be the most heart-wrenching lesson of all.

I had to put an end to my automatic response and weak stomach. Danny would be coming home soon, and I would have to help him. I desperately wanted to; I met with the nurse several times and read the literature daily, forcing myself to look at the pictures to help me overcome this problem. The surgery was already giving him relief, so for that I was grateful. My squeamish stomach took over a month to settle down, and by the time Danny was home I had mastered my greatest challenge. Thank you, God.

Today is Valentine's Day, the day of love. I tried not to let the recent news spoil this day; it was one of our favorite holidays. I went to the photo shop, and to my surprise, on display in the window was our wedding picture. They had it in the shape of a huge heart, and there were people gathered in front of the store admiring it. It was a magnificent photo of us standing by the stream, and for a few moments I was taken back in time when life was so vibrant and pure. People around me quickly recognized that I was the bride and they had wonderful things to say to me, tears started streaming down my face as I started to crumble and abruptly left!

When I returned to the hospital, I pulled myself together as I shared the story with Danny, and suddenly the recent news seemed a million miles away! Love really does conquer all. Danny loved the picture of me that I gave to him as his gift, and we enjoyed a little champagne. Danny felt terrible because he could not get me a present, and I told him that that he already did just by being with me. We spent a quiet evening listening to jazz and reading a book of love poems to each other.

Over the next few days, many visitors flocked to the hospital. Greg and Sharon were visiting us on a daily basis. Danny and Greg were very close, and his spirited, charismatic wife always brought a smile to my face. Sharon used to tell me that she hated hospitals and was the most unlikely person to be able to give me support and strength. The two of us had become very close. She had come to visit us since day one, and I relished her advice and strong wisdom. I was quickly learning that I had many angels that gave me strength.

Danny and I had many somber conversations in the following days. We talked about the journey we were on and how he felt like the end of his life was coming. Strange how I never had to tell him what the doctors predicted; somehow he always knew. He wanted to finalize the plans we had laid the groundwork for. He told me he was on borrowed time. I used our upcoming trip to Florida to brighten his spirit and give him something to look forward to. I was so happy when Marie came into town to visit, we had a wonderful time, her humor, wisdom and love was exactly what I needed.

Over the next few weeks, all of my energy was focused on Danny and repairing the distance between us. Since our wedding, he had felt like he was failing and now that emotion was amplified because of the surgery. He hated his body, and he hated needing me so much. He started becoming very angry. He refused to see anyone or take phone calls. I knew it was because his condition was getting worse: The pain was agonizing for him. I tried not letting what he said affect my love for him. After all, could you really blame him? I couldn't. It was very difficult for me; I was being forced to live in two separate worlds. Shortly after that he told me he wanted to die and asked for my help, and when I said no he took matters into his own hands. He opened up a box of duragesic patches and stuck them all over his body. I thank God that I discovered the empty box soon after he had put them on. I knew that they contained enough morphine to probably kill him or at least induce a coma in his weakened condition.

This was a desperate cry for help. I climbed in bed with him and held him in my arms, and he started crying hysterically like he had never done before. I started peeling off the patches and asked him if the angels would want this to happen. He said, "No, it's not time for me yet." I told him that I knew how very frustrated he was but he had to fight, and I wanted to know what the real problem was that would make him want to take his life. He told me it was the knife-stabbing pains in his side that wouldn't go away. I made him realize that I had done everything humanly possible to help him and that I would never help him take his life, that it was cruel for him to hold that against me. I asked him if stronger medication might ease the gripping pain, and he agreed that he needed something stronger. I immediately went to see his doctor to inform him of the latest turn of events, and he changed Danny's medication. I was satisfied.

The stronger medication was the answer to our prayer, and I would improve his mood by renting funny movies we loved. Whoopi Goldberg was his ultimate favorite entertainer! Music videos and comedies were our top picks. Blockbuster Video was my new best friend. I would rent four and five movies a day. I tried filling his days with laughter, and I made him have our friends over and let people back into his life. Doug would come over as much as he could, his worldwide business travels kept him on the go. Danny missed him; they had a one-of-a-kind friendship. They were awesome friends. Danny was beyond angry about one day possibly not playing the guitar or a fierce game of racquetball with him. Danny tried to ease ours nerves with his humor. Whatever it took to boost his spirits, we did. There was plenty of mood-food to keep a person festive.

It was the smallest things that I did for him that impacted his emotional well-being the most. Every morning I gave him fresh flowers on his breakfast tray, and we would sit outside on our patio enjoying the morning sunshine. We would squeeze in a game of darts if he was feeling up to it. He started playing his guitar again, and he finally was becoming less aggressive. He was adjusting to his surgery and the limitations that surrounded it. His dreams were increasingly more vivid, and they were about death. One evening in particular that I recall, I woke to sounds of Danny talking: He was speaking in a language that I had never heard before. The room was enveloped in a thick dark smoke, and I couldn't move. I thought he was having a nightmare, when in fact, he later told me that the angels showed him what death was like. I was frightened, because in the past I had always been allowed to witness the experience. Not this time. It was as if I was restrained in bed. I tried to reach over and touch him, but I couldn't move. It felt like I was being held down. I could only see the dark smoke lingering around the bed. Danny was speaking in a calm voice.

After that experience, Danny asked me to read his Bible to him about Heaven and death to help reinforce what he had seen. I wanted him to focus on what was ahead instead of what he thought he was losing. We had many conversations about the strange encounter. It helped us both to better understand the transition that would take place. I tried not to be emotional with him, and I tried to pray without panic.

It was time for chemotherapy again, and a portable catheter was placed in his chest. Danny was very happy to be able to have chemo in the doctor's office. I would bring him treats and read funny stories to him so that his body would be relaxed and able to accept the chemotherapy better. I had to shift his focus in order for the internal healing process to work better. Doug would come by full of life and laughter, and it brought a smile to Danny's face each and every time. Doug didn't care if the only thing he could do for Danny was to carry a tray of food for him. Doug just wanted Danny to know he was there with him, feeling the pain and anguish as if it were happening to him. The two of them had countless conversations about each of our futures. I just wanted Danny to be in very good spirits by the end of the treatment, not planning Death 101. Even though he was weak, he wanted to play golf. He had recovered from the surgery, and by Easter his pain was under control and we were trying to enjoy spring to the fullest. He never ceased to amaze me: It was wonderful that through the entire trauma we learned to take what life had in store but never to look down. Death seemed a million miles away as we planned our trip the following month to visit his daughter.

Danny desperately wanted to play golf again even though he had lost an enormous amount of weight, but his energy and appetite were on the rise. I surprised Danny by calling my mom and asking her to take him golfing. I packed them a lunch, and off they went. They were both like little kids, full of excitement to be able to go to the golf course. The doctors were stunned at the progress he was making; they tried to give me credit for his improvement and for keeping him so well adjusted. God and Danny deserved the praise. He left me in complete awe with his determination and zest. The admiration that I felt for him filled me with jubilation.

I was so pleased that Danny was able to enjoy golf again. It was very inspiring for him to be outside with the deer roaming and the sunshine beaming down. From the first day he picked up his clubs, it was impossible to keep him off of the course. He had been shattered when the doctors told him that after the surgery he wouldn't be able to play any longer. He loved proving them wrong, which he did time and time again. After all, he was supposed to be dead by now. While Danny was golfing, I used the time for myself, indulging in my favorite passion: ballet. I missed dancing everyday, and for me it was the perfect therapy that my soul craved.

By the first week of May we were very excited to be celebrating our one-year anniversary with his daughter and Connie. We were all due for some serious fun in the Florida sun! I would have preferred that Danny and I fly to Orlando, but he had other plans. He wanted to see the country, so we rented a Cadillac and made our way to Florida. I was very worried that the drive would be miserable for him, but he loved it! His pain was minimal, and we stopped along the way to enjoy the beauty of each state. It was what we both needed. The escape was the perfect mood booster for us. We had great conversations and reflected on our wedding and honeymoon. We were very proud of ourselves to have made it this far after being told repeatedly that Danny would never be alive to celebrate our first anniversary. Bravo to us! Thank you, God!

From the moment we arrived, his daughter could hardly contain her excitement to see her dad again. Danny and I were quite impressed at how well she had been handling the news of his diagnosis. I credit Connie for maintaining her well-being. We had a fabulous time, went to the beach, shopped, and of course ate incredible food.

Danny was feeling great: He played golf and we stayed up late every night sharing stories, drinking champagne, and laughing our heads off. I think Danny was regretting that Connie and I had become such good friends as we talked about him until the wee hours of the morning. All in good fun, of course!

With our visit ending in a couple of days, Danny turned to a serious topic: preparing and planning for his daughter to someday be without a father. We never lost sight of the fact that the tumors in the liver were growing, and we knew that it could eventually take his life. Danny wanted to cover every possibility.

While Danny was planning things, he decided this would be a good time for him to inform me which of our friends I could date and who I would marry. He was dead serious! Forcefully blunt and very matter-of-fact. This was a heated conversation, and to make matters worse we were just leaving Florida, driving! Once I gained my composure, I was pretty annoyed with his plans. He absolutely would not let this go. I asked him if he had told our friends that he was planning their lives. What on earth would you say? He said the person or people that need to know will! He was very calm and had no hesitation to make this happen. Thoughts were discussed, and with that being said, our conversations that followed were never the same.

The conversations we had were spinning in my mind, and this was not how I wanted to end our vacation. We left Florida with heavy hearts and many tears. Danny told me that he knew that was probably the last time he would ever see his daughter again. We had only been on the road a little while when the flood of emotions came pouring out: It was overwhelming for Danny. The anger and frustration were setting in quickly, and Danny was distraught. He hated being on the road, and he failed to tell me that he had taken all of his pain pills. Here we were hundreds of miles away from home; I was driving in the pouring rain, and Danny was in agonizing pain.

The one thing that gave him comfort was the kitten he gave me for our anniversary while we were there. We named him Orlando (for obvious reasons). He curled up in Danny's arms the entire drive home, and he helped Danny to stay calm. Orlando was an adorable kitten. I knew why Danny wanted me to have him, I thought it was very sweet. He did make the drive home a little more tolerable, even though it was grueling and tedious. I tried to keep the conversation light.

Miracles Can Be in Motion

~

We had little time to adjust to being back home before it was time for chemotherapy again. I tried not to let our recent conversations frustrate me, but it was challenging and very odd when I would see our friends who Danny had made these plans for. I know it was obvious I was behaving strangely, the dynamic of our marriage had changed and the relationships within our inner-circle had shifted. Having to spend more time at the hospital and doctor's office than we had in our own home was creating its own set of problems. Everyday was a new adventure for us, and with the tumors growing out of control I had to be extra creative in finding ways to keep his spirits up. I tried not to focus on what I can't change, but rather what I could. I wanted our environment to be as serene as possible; I wanted life to be the focus. I moved most of the medications that were not essential to the guest bathroom so that he would not be overwhelmed by the abundance of pill bottles and boxes. When he needed his medication, I would bring them to him. I would buy him new clothes almost every other week to keep up with his rapid weight loss. I would cut the sizing tags out so that he would not focus on his severe weight loss, and I would move all of the larger sizes into the guest bedroom closet so that it would not be a constant reminder. When I shopped for him I made certain that I bought the exact same thing in smaller sizes. He loved to wear Dockers, and I never had any problem finding the pants in the same color and style. I never told him what I was doing. That would have defeated the purpose of what I was accomplishing. Having an entire closet full of clothes that could no longer be worn and seeing the enormous amount of medical supplies as well as medication everyday would become difficult for Danny to handle. I would do things in a subtle way over months so that he would not become aware of what I was doing.

When it was time for chemotherapy again, Danny was able to have a portable pack and have his treatment at home. I had to learn how to operate the pump and change the lines and tubes for him. Vicki, our nurse, trained me, and I found it challenging and scary to say the least; but I knew Danny wanted to be able to stay home, so I mastered it. I loved the idea, but the responsibility was on my shoulders if it was going to be possible. Vicki is a very special nurse; both Danny and I loved her very much. She brought the humanity and compassion back into the inhumane world of cancer. Danny and I became very close to her, and a special bond developed between us that would last a lifetime. We depended on her greatly, I was so thankful that she gave us her home phone number in case of an emergency, and she came into the office after hours and on weekends to help us. Definitely another one of God's special angels!

Danny loved being at home, and it helped keep him in better spirits. Friends would come over to visit and offer any help they could. Karen was quickly becoming my rock, I needed her insight and she unselfishly gave me her love, time, and exuberance! The severity of the cancer was obvious and Danny and I were both glad when this treatment came to an end. We were relieved that we had overcome another hurdle. I felt like I had been put through a crash course in Nursing 101.

With June almost here, we were at the one-year mark of the diagnosis, and his liver was starting to fail. Tests revealed that it would soon be non-functional. That was the reality that we were facing. We did everything in our power to sustain his life, but his appetite was fluctuating and the medication was again increased. I gave Danny massages at least five times a day, and I would have him focus on my heartbeat to help control his sporadic breathing. I would lead him into meditation and mentally take him on a journey to a healthier, happier time, usually back to the golf course or the beach. Orlando would lie next to him every moment, and the purring helped to keep Danny serene. I never would have imagined how much positive impact a pet could have until I saw it with my own eyes.

By mid-June it was time for chemotherapy again. This treatment was very hard on him. Each day he was in enormous pain and not able to sleep much. We lived in the bedroom and spent the rest of the month alone. I still gave him fresh flowers and I would read to him. We filled our days watching funny movies and listening to music. Danny should have been put in the hospital, but he begged me to let him stay at home. We had problems with the chemo lines on the pump; while he was sleeping they snapped and spilled chemotherapy all over the floor. Thank goodness I had our nurse Vicki's phone number. I called her in a panic at 5 a.m., and she told me how to replace the lines. Danny was terrified, and the following night when it happened again while he was sleeping, he became too afraid to fall asleep. She met us at the office and gave us replacement lines, the ones we used had a defect from the manufacturer. Danny was livid. It was hard on him to have such unexpected things happen.

Danny was very weak and frail, and his body was starting to swell. He was getting much worse. We had no control over what God had planned for us, and it was painfully obvious that Danny was rapidly losing his fight. Even though I was becoming very sick, it was still my mission to make him laugh even though I was living in two very different worlds. I tried not to be consumed with guilt about being the one able to go on and have a life as opposed to lying in the hospital bed hooked up to a chemo pump. Our friends were experiencing conflicting emotions as well, a couple of them more so than the others.

The only fireworks we saw that 4th of July were from our bedroom window. Danny was too exhausted too enjoy the holiday, but I did run around the bedroom with sparklers blazing! Danny got a kick out of it, and we spent the rest of the evening sipping champagne while he tried to play his guitar.

After that night, Danny again was having very vivid dreams. He would tell me about his conversations with the angels; we talked about what they would show him. We believed that death was a transition from one journey to the next. When the angels would appear there were no more of the white pulsating lights—instead it would be the dark smoke lingering all around us like before. Danny told me they were helping him to prepare for leaving this phase of his existence.

With all of the other experiences we had been through, I fully believed him and trusted my instinct to guide me. My dreams were more of flashbacks in nature. I would be shown a funeral service and given insight on how I should cope and carry on. I knew that in my heart and soul God was walking hand in hand with us. A friend of ours came to me when he started having strange dreams about Danny and I, and he too was being shown by a higher power what was in store. I found it very comforting that his closest friends loved Danny so much that it was transcending to the heavens. We were definitely not alone on our journey.

With my birthday here once again, I was feeling more like 77 than 27. Our experiences gave me peace of mind and re-enforced my unconditional love for Danny. I knew that he would always be with me. He told me that the angels showed him the way.

Danny's courage and determination left me speechless once again. I watched in silence from a crack in the door as Danny dragged a chair into the kitchen and with his chemo pump clicking away, began icing the cake he had baked for me. He was very weak and pale, I knew that he was in an enormous amount of pain, but he was able to put it aside and we enjoyed a wonderful day at my mother's house. Danny was in good spirits and focused on my birthday to ease the pain. I knew this would probably be the last cake he would ever create for me; it was a very bittersweet realization.

Over the next few days Danny's condition was getting much worse! His body started swelling due to the toxins building in his system. His legs were so huge that even trying to wear socks was impossible; he had a raging fever and the chemotherapy had to be stopped in mid-stream. We found ourselves back at the doctor's office daily, and by mid-July the news we had been so fortunate to avoid had become a shattering reality. Dr. Campos told us that there was nothing more that could be done, and with tears welling up in his eyes he told us that Danny had only a few weeks at the most to live.

Danny was so strong, he kissed me and gave me a hug and begged me not to cry. I turned white as the wall and the room started to spin. I made a quick exit to the bathroom and completely fell apart. I tried to calm myself by focusing on the angels and all of the extraordinary experiences that Danny and I were blessed with. I regained my composure and went down to admitting to check Danny in. The hospital staff had been so supportive to us that this news was devastating for them as well.

Danny had always said that he did not wish to be in the hospital when he took his last breath and that he only wanted me by his side. His condition was so extreme, his skin and eyes were bright yellow and he was vomiting bright green bile. He weighed only 100 pounds. He was badly bruised from all of the shots, and he was more than ready for the agony to come to an end!

I found enormous comfort in my nightly visits with the hospital greeter, Kenneth. He always had words of wisdom for me, and he had a natural grace and warmth about him, his is eyes had a wonderful sparkle. He was my shoulder to cry on in the late hours of the night, and his smile and sweet voice greeted me daily, (he reminded me of Morgan Freeman) he was a blessing to me.

Calling our friends and family was so heartbreaking. With each call I made I became more emotional. I could barely speak as I phoned Doug. He came to hospital—I needed his strength and support, I trusted him completely, and he was my rock on this mountain heaped with torment. The impact was hitting me full force. Danny refused to let me call his family. I begged him and tried to explain to him that if he died and they didn't know until it was too late, that they would never forgive me! Quite frankly, I couldn't blame them. Danny didn't care. He made me promise. After hours of fighting, I gave in to his wishes. I asked God to forgive me. I knew what Danny was doing was wrong, and in his heart he knew it as well. How do you find the words to say goodbye to your family when your birthday is just around the corner? Danny refused to dwell on the trauma.

Friends and co-workers rushed to the hospital, and we were once again overwhelmed by the love and care we were shown. Everyone who came to visit had a positive, upbeat attitude. Danny loved having visitors and, even though he was very weak, his sense of humor was alive and well. We were lucky to have such wonderful people around us. All of our friends who were in our wedding made our days tolerable, even if it was devastatingly bittersweet. Greg and Sharon would visit us daily. She still claimed that she had a weak stomach for hospitals. I told her that she should consider being a caregiver; since she had shown us such love and compassion and brought us such comfort, I felt that she had missed her calling.

With August here it was Danny's 39th birthday, and he was not doing well at all. He was getting much worse. The yellowing of his skin was very dramatic, and he had lost another 25 pounds. Danny tried not to let his condition dampen his spirits; we had a terrific celebration with a few friends and my family. He loved the games, toys and books that he was given. I gave Danny a very special present; I contacted the International Star Registry in Switzerland and reserved a star in the Leo constellation in his name. They sent Danny the official documents and a star chart with his coordinates. I told him that I would always know where to find him in the heavens above. Danny was moved beyond words. I reminded him that our friendship and love for each other was the ultimate gift!

During the next several days, Danny's condition was becoming critical. I was informed that Danny had maybe a week or two at the most to live. He would slip into a coma and would be alive only a day or two after that. I was told to start preparing myself for that moment. It was happening. The life I tried so desperately to save was slipping away. I was given the papers Danny and I were to sign stating that no life support or extreme measures would be taken. Do Not Resuscitate.

I gave Danny the papers. We were both sobbing. It was the most painful moment I had ever experienced in my life. "This is for the best," he said, tears streaming down his face. "I can't live on machines. I want this to be over. I want to be free of pain and agony. I want peace." He kissed me, and I snuggled in his bed and spent the entire night reading love poems to him and gently caressing his sweet face.

As Danny's illness progressed, I began to get sick. This ordeal was too much for my body to take—my health went straight into the toilet. Dr. Campos warned me to take better care of myself. I wasn't sleeping much and I had no appetite. I was very thin and exhausted from this rollercoaster ride from Hell. I thought I would be able to take care of myself after things calmed down. Reality proved to foil my well-laid plan, and I found myself needing the doctor's care. I was diagnosed with pneumonia and a fever of 103 degrees. I was ordered to leave Danny. He could not be exposed to my illness. It felt like my heart was being ripped out! I became very angry from this unfortunate turn of events.

I begged my doctor to give me anything and everything to help get me well. I needed bed rest, food, and B-12 shots. To make matters worse, I completely lost my voice. I had to rely on my mom and our friends for reports on Danny. I felt helpless; I couldn't stand being away from Danny at this critical point in his life. I had no choice but to rest and mend myself. It took me almost a week before I was able to return to the hospital. Talk about a nightmare!

Time was quickly passing, and with the end of August almost here Danny was barely alive. It was devastating to see him in this state. I remembered watching him play racquetball with Doug and Pat. The vitality and energy he once had was now completely vanished. His acceptance of his illness gave him the courage to face his mortality. He drew strength from his belief in God, and the angels helped him every step of the way.

One evening Danny and I started talking, He asked me what I was going to wear to his funeral. He smiled and said, "Don't cry, be strong. I want you to dress for me. I'll be watching, and I don't want to see you in some ugly potato sack. I want you to wear something beautiful with lace and beads and a hat." I explained that I was not attending a gala. "You are young, beautiful, and sexy. Do this one last thing for me, please." How could I refuse? The next day I asked Sharon to go shopping with me, I purchased two black velvet evening suits trimmed with lace and beads and a velvet hat, just like Danny had asked me to do. I had to put my emotions on autopilot so that I wouldn't break down. One daunting task always seemed to lead to another, always pointing me towards the reality of death.

Every evening I would sit in a chair next to Danny's bed. I would hold his hand while he slept. His body was too bruised to give him the massages that he loved so much, it was my way of staying close to him. We had many quiet conversations in the days that followed.

One of the most poignant conversations Danny and I had was on August 25. "The end is almost here for me," he said. In a soft weak voice he continued, "Soon I will not be able to talk to you anymore, and I want to take this time to tell what you have brought to my life. I could have never asked for a better wife or best friend. The sacrifices that you have made for me and the compassion that you have shown me fill me with love." He apologized to me for all of the fighting and his stubborn and feisty ways. I told him that I knew how much he loved me and as for the fighting. I looked past the emotions. Danny told me that on the day he married me his life became complete. I knew that our friendship and love would transcend through the grave.

August 26th—this day would prove to bring no good news. The morphine had to be increased again: He was in agonizing pain. I would shift his focus by leading him through meditation; he would listen to my heartbeat as I spoke softly. We didn't sleep much. Danny was very concerned about me and how I would carry on with my life. He told me to get married again. He always said I had too much love inside not to share it. Tears were pouring down our faces. Danny wanted to make things easier for me, and he thought that if he gave me his blessing I would carry on and not let one day go by without living my life to the fullest. Life is too short, and you can't get love if you don't give love.

August 27th—we were off to a rocky start as the morphine had to be increased again. Danny was taking so much medication for his pain that it was alarming. He was taking pills, wearing duragesic patches, and he had the IV pump for pain. Nothing could seem to relieve his pain. Danny was having very vivid dreams about death, and I could feel my soul start to crumble. I still would light the fragrant candles and play soft jazz music for him to keep a serene environment. Danny was still very worried about how his death would affect me. He was very persistent about the plans he had made for me'

That evening we had another conversation about his plans for my life, he pulled out his list of all of our single men friends. He had made notes in the margins. Once again I was stunned; he wanted a progress report and again made his decisions and conversations known. I didn't know whether to cry or laugh! Danny was serious about the issue; he said he loved me so much he wanted to make certain that he helped me to carry on with my life. He proceeded once again to give me his thoughts on his list.

Another concern that Danny had was my career. He knew that I was helping other families who were facing the same situation we were. I would share tips with them and music and a few books. You can't spend so much time surrounded by the same people without getting to know them. The only difference was my age: Danny and I were the youngest people on the second floor. It was normal that they were curious as to how we dealt with the diagnosis. You could smell our candles from the hall and hear the music, so of course they wanted to do anything they could for their family members. The nurses would always see me giving Danny massages. One even calculated that in one year I gave Danny 5,000 massages.

Danny told me that I could help people because I was caring, loving and had the courage and strength to give of myself unselfishly. Danny was definitely going to plan all phases of my life whether I was ready for it or not. I wanted him to concentrate on things that would make him smile. I would write messages to him in lipstick on the bathroom mirror so that when he looked at himself, instead of seeing the physical appearance, he would see the love I had for him. When I was working I would leave love notes on his food in the refrigerator and rose petals on his pillow. Love is the greatest motivator of creativity. When you love with your heart and soul, you always find a window instead of a closed door! I know he was preparing for the end, but I tried my best to make him laugh and forget about everything.

Tranquility

~

August 28th—I begged Danny to let me call his family, but he flatly refused. "You can call them after I'm gone," he replied sharply. There was no reasoning with him on this topic; I told him that it was wrong to do this to them and that I would have to live with this for the rest of my life, that I wouldn't be able to. Against his wishes I picked up the phone and dialed his Mother's number. Danny was so furious with me that he knocked the phone to the floor. I couldn't risk going against something he felt so strongly about anymore. My heart-ached.

Later in the day the morphine had to be increased again, and Danny had stopped eating. He told me that nothing tasted good and he had no desire for food anymore. I knew the end was very near, and even though he couldn't get out of bed or barely speak, he still managed to enjoy the time with our friends. It was becoming more difficult for the emotions to be checked at the door. The images left a stinging pain in my soul. Like every night before this one, I held his hand while he rested. His breathing was very hard. I didn't know when the time would come, so I refused to let my panic hinder my thoughts and actions. I knew that when he did finally slip into a coma that it wouldn't be much longer.

August 29th—the morphine was increased yet again. We had a peaceful day. My mom spent the afternoon with us. With me being so sick it was very difficult to make phone calls, as I still had no voice. Pat and Cindy dropped in that evening and brought us prayer books and other special gifts. It was a very emotional visit. I felt a numbing exhaustion sweep over me as I lay with Danny later that night, and finally in the wee hours of the morning Danny was able to sleep.

August 30th—I awoke to the sound of his doctor explaining to Danny why he couldn't have any more chemotherapy and what was happening. I could barely hear Danny; he was wheezing and gasping for air. He asked to see me in private. I already knew what the conversation would be about. I sat motionless as he held my hands; the words tumbled out of his mouth and crashed into my soul like a tidal wave. He told me that Danny was barely hanging on, fighting with all of his might to stay alive. I couldn't choke back the tears as he told me that Danny had a day to live at the most. I could feel my soul slipping away and I felt useless. He told me what a lucky man Danny was to have a wife who loved him so much. He wished his other patients had just an ounce of my courage and strength; I told him again I did not feel so strong or brave. "Danny would have died along time ago if you weren't in his life," he stated quietly. He continued, trying to control his emotions as he spoke. "I have seen many of my patients whose spouse has left them because they couldn't handle the pressure, but you stood by Danny and improved his quality of life." He gave me a hug and told me how much he admired me. He told me that Danny was clinging to life and I needed to give him my blessing and let him know that it was time for him to let go.

I knew that his doctor was right, and now I had to find the words and insight to tell him. I went outside to the courtyard to gather my thoughts: I wanted to choose my words and phrasing carefully. I couldn't walk back in the room and just say Okay, Danny, go ahead and die. I'll be fine. He deserved better than that. I visualized myself lying there and what words would bring me peace and comfort and allow me to let go. This was one situation in which I didn't have insight. I had to speak from my heart, have his interests and concerns in mind, and allay his fears about my well-being and ability to continue on. This would be the greatest task I would ever have to perform and truly the most enriching. It was one conversation that needed to bring me the greatest Tranquility and not silence.

I picked some flowers from the courtyard garden to give to Danny. I took a deep breath and briefly went over in my mind what I wanted to say to him. I walked into the room and Danny smiled. I winked at him and blew him a kiss as I walked over to his bed. I lowered the railing on the bed and started caressing his face with one of the roses, and Danny asked me about having chemotherapy. I started softly kissing his sweet face and whispering in his ear. "Danny, I want you to rest now, I know how tired you are." He nodded his head yes. "It's time for you to go and play with the angels."

He again nodded yes, squeezed my hand and whispered, "I love you."

"I love you with all my heart. That's why I want you to continue your journey. You don't need anymore treatments or shots. God is waiting to help you. He wants you to be healthy and pain free." Danny smiled and said, "No more pain," and I nodded. "That's right, no more pain. But he can't help you if you stay here with me, and besides, how will you know what the donuts taste like in heaven if you're here?" Danny chuckled. "But don't feed the angels too many or they won't be able to fly." Danny's eyes lit up.

I continued on. "It is a glorious day outside, the sun is shining; the sky is bright blue, just like in the Bahamas. It's a perfect day to travel. I want you to promise me that you will dance in the heavens above and always know that our love can never leave your soul, you will take it with you, all the love I have for you. He winked and nodded yes. "Every moment we have ever spent together is woven into my heart, and when you see God tell him how much love, joy, and laughter you have given me. On our wedding day an eternal flame was ignited in my soul that will guide me for the rest of my life." The tears were gently streaming down Danny's face as he kissed my hand. "Even though I can't predict my future, it is your help that gave me the wisdom and love to continue on my journey. Now it is time for you to rest. You'll need your strength to go and receive your angel wings." I kissed him and thanked him; Danny told me again how much he loved me.

We barely finished our conversation before the phone started ringing. It was Danny's sister. She asked to speak to Danny. I told her that he was not able to talk on the phone. She told me that they were coming into town. Danny started shaking his head and he kept saying no, tell them no. I tried to explain to her that Danny really did not want any visitors, I was being put in a terrible position by Danny and I hated it. I told her to please try to be strong for Danny's sake, and that he was very sick and weak. I knew this visit would be very traumatic for them.

I tried to call my mom, but she was on the golf course. I called as many of our friends as I could to have them come to the hospital. I knew it would be an ordeal, and I had no energy for this battle. I called Doug to tell him the devastating news about Danny's condition; he knew what was coming before I said a word. I knew he wanted to keep his thoughts and memories of his friendship with Danny whole, not of death and trauma, but I needed him, and in spite of his emotional state he came to the hospital.

Danny's family should be here with him, I was hoping that for Danny's well-being it would be a peaceful time for each of them. But on the other hand I knew that their attitude would greatly affect him, and he did not need to be challenged in any way. I did my best to pull myself together and shifted my focus to Danny: I wanted him to remain in good spirits.

It was late in the day when his family arrived, and tensions were on high voltage. They barely spoke to me when they entered the room, Danny started to break down. Just a short time ago he had been so peaceful and in such good spirits.

I could sense that a heated discussion was on the horizon as his sister asked to speak to me outside the room. The minute we were in the hallway she started screaming at me. I already had several strikes against me since I was so sick. Trying to talk with no voice was almost impossible for me.

"That's my brother in there dying, and you weren't even going to call us," she shouted. I tried to explain that Danny wouldn't let me, but she wasn't listening. I pleaded with her to lower her voice, the nurses told her to be quiet, as were the patients around us, I begged her to calm down, and finally I started to walk away when she grabbed me and a struggle broke out between us! "You're just the wife!" she yelled. "We are his family, not you! Who the hell do you think you are keeping us away from him?"

I exploded, "I had to respect his wishes." The nurses came running down the hall when they saw us fighting. I broke free from her grip and fell against the wall. That was the straw that broke the camel's back. I had the nurses call Security and they were removed from the floor. I was trembling from head to toe.

I called the country club where my mom was playing golf. I asked to have her come to the hospital right away. I told them that Danny was dying but to please not tell mom, because she had a very long drive to the hospital and I wanted her there in one piece.

Our friends Sharon and Greg arrived just in time to help me regain my composure. Sharon sat with me and helped me to calm down, while Greg went in to see Danny. I told them what had just happened and that Danny needed cheering up. Having Sharon with me was an added strength that I desperately needed—she brought an enormous amount of love and friendship to my life when it was the darkest. A truly compassionate gift from the heavens above. I was very blessed.

As the hours passed, Danny was becoming weaker, and he couldn't even whisper anymore. Danny's brother and his wife arrived along with Danny's father. I let them into the room, I wanted no more fighting. Upon seeing his father, Danny became very emotional. I was glad to see his brother and wife but quite stunned to see his father. His brother's wife and I had many conversations over the past several months, and she had always been very understanding and supportive. I enjoyed spending time with her.

By the time Doug arrived, Danny was barely breathing. He was gradually slipping away. I left the room to go and see his mother and sister and try to make them understand why I couldn't go against Danny's wishes. Again tempers were flaring as I was trying to defend my actions. Finally I had enough and returned to the room.

The moment I walked back in, Danny started choking and gasping for air. Doug and his brother helped him to sit up, hoping it would help him to breathe. I called for the nurse, and when she entered the room she did nothing. I started to leave the room to go and get the rest of his family, but I overheard the nurses in the hallway discussing that Danny was dying; they were horrified when they saw me standing there. I was shattered as I ran back into the room.

We gathered around his bed. I held his hand and told him how much I loved him. Danny took one more breath and the life I so desperately wanted to save, was Over. I crushed my body into Doug's and clung to him, I could feel his heartbeat penetrating my body and his breath washing through me. I had life pumping through my body on one side and death on the other! Danny's sister in law started singing a beautiful hymn; everyone was clinging to each other. At last Danny was with the angels that he spoke of. I stood over him, frozen. All I recall is the sound of silence as I squeezed Doug's hands into mine. Feeling in my heart that God was with us on this journey. Trying to convince and remind myself to be strong, that I was prepared for this. Danny had prepared me for this, and that I wasn't alone.

I left the room and went outside to the garden in the courtyard. I felt like my entire world was in shambles. My life had been blown apart and all I could do was to be grateful that I was given the chance to experience unconditional love. I recalled every second of every day that I spent with Danny was now becoming a precious memory of a life I cherished. There were no more treatments or shots to endure and no more pain. He was with God, and I prayed that knowing that would light my path. The tranquility that Danny so desperately wanted was finally his. My tranquility would not come so easy! This was the last Bible passage that Danny had read.

Psalm 23

The Lord is my shepherd, I shall not want.
He makes me lie down in green pastures;
He leads me beside still waters.
He restores my soul;
He guides me in the paths of righteousness for His name's sake.
Even though I walk through the valley of the shadow of Death,
I fear no evil, for Thou art with me;
Thy rod and Thy staff, they comfort me.
Thou dost prepare a table before me
In the presence of my enemies;
Thou hast anointed my head with oil;
My cup overflows.
Surely goodness and loving kindness will follow me all the days of my life,
And I will dwell in the house of the Lord.

NEW AMERICAN STANDARD BIBLE: Concordance

I was devastated as I stood outside the hospital staring up at that sky in shock. Even with Doug by my side, it felt as though nothing I could have done would have prepared me for this incredible sense of loss. The plans that Danny and I had made in preparation for this moment made it easier to cope with the physical tasks, but the numbing pain in my soul and crushed spirit were in God's hands. My mother still had not arrived and I was more than ready to leave. Doug and Greg finished packing Danny's things while Sharon stayed with me.

I don't remember who drove me home or where my car was. Everything was spinning out of control in my mind. I kept hearing Danny's voice telling me to be strong. I had to focus on finishing the funeral arrangements; I had many calls to make and a memorial service to plan. I was feeling very overwhelmed and isolated.

As soon as I got home, I tried to call Danny's son, but there was no answer. I knew he would come by or call. The last time I had seen him was several months before, when he came to see his dad in the hospital. It was a short visit; I knew he was having an extremely difficult time coping with his father's illness.

My mind was reeling as I tried to focus on calling Connie, and I tried to gather my thoughts. I knew there would be no easy way. The minute Connie heard my voice, she knew that something terrible had happened. I shared Danny's last day with her moment by moment. I told her how much Danny loved her. It was a very agonizing conversation. She was grief-stricken and the emotional loss hit me like a rogue ocean wave!

When I returned to the living room, my mom had finally arrived. Doug and Danny's family had also arrived. We were all crying, it was heartbreaking. His sister gave me a hug and we apologized to each other for all of the fighting. I told her how sorry I was and that I didn't want to fight anymore. They thanked me for letting them call a priest, it gave them comfort. I shared with them the arrangements that Danny wanted and were already made. I would like to be able to say that there was no more fighting, but that would not be the case as his mother turned her sorrow and grief into rage against me. "Who the hell do you think you are keeping me from my son?" She was screaming at me and pushed me against the window. Emotions were very tense as we exchanged words. I had finally had enough.

I made it very clear that my patience had run out. Danny's sister, mom, and I went into the bedroom to choose a suit for Danny to be buried in. It took every ounce of strength not to fall apart when I saw all of his clothes in the closet. I quickly laid out a black suit and his favorite tie. Mom started to choke back the tears and I begged her to be strong: I knew that once she started to cry I would fall apart. I had to stay focused on the task at hand; I could not allow myself to crumble.

After all of the fighting that had gone on that day, I was left feeling raw and exhausted, so when my mom expressed that she was feeling left out and hurt, I was at a loss for words—we still had to plan the memorial service and funeral. She was the only family member I had by my side, and she left me. I was stunned, puzzled, and bewildered. I needed and wanted her support.

I had to push the incident with mom aside as I sat with Danny's family. My patience was very short as they told me what church and type of funeral service they wanted. I reminded them of Danny's wishes, rather than argue, I agreed to every last detail, and within minutes it was done and I said my good-byes and at last had peace. I could finally start to absorb the emotionally draining events of the day that were so devastating for me. My emotions left me crumpled on the bathroom floor wailing. I begged God to help me. "Come be with me!" I cried out to him, over and over, "Send the angels back! I need them, I need them," I shouted out. "I need You, help me! Help me, God, I can't do this, I can't do this I shouted over and over." And he answered me. "I AM WITH YOU ALWAYS."

All throughout the night I had very strange experiences. The television would turn off by itself and every clock in the house stopped running. The answering machine would come on by itself and play Danny's message. It was shocking to hear his voice. I tried to rest, but it was impossible. I was very sick. I had a high fever and I was exhausted.

The next day was extremely difficult. I still had not heard from my mom, so I had to finish the arrangements by myself. All day long I could hear Danny's voice coaching me, and Doug was having similar experiences as well and extremely powerful dreams! By late that day I collapsed on the bed consumed by illness, grief, and anger towards the people who were supposed to love and support me. I watched our wedding video. It brought me comfort to see Danny so happy. Our close friend, Jim, filmed the ceremony for us. He did a great job, considering the wind was gusting and howling, making filming very challenging. I refused to let his death overshadow or tarnish our beautiful wedding. Early in the evening friends came by to help me finish the plans. They helped me sort and cut pictures for a tribute for Danny. It was actually a nice evening, and the pictures that were chosen brought back great memories for all of us.

I tried to sleep, but my attempt was futile. I could not shut my mind off. It was like I was engulfed in a sea of memories and conflicting emotions!

With the sun rising, I found myself in need of emergency dental service. The term medical mishap came to mind. I still had not heard from my mom, and it being a weekday, I had no choice but to drive myself across town. Having a root canal done combined with the fever and exhaustion was sheer torture, but I had no choice. The only saving grace was that I had my two friends flying in later that day. The support that they had shown me was a godsend. Cindy and Marie were my closest friends, I needed their strength and love.

The next morning was excruciating; I stood frozen in front of the mirror as I recalled the conversation that Danny and I had had regarding this moment. "I don't want you wearing some old potato sack," I could hear him saying. I cut the tags off the beaded evening suit and donned the hat; the tears were streaming down my face as I pulled the veil down. I sat numb in the limousine. My friends did their best to help me. I reflected on every detail of my life with Danny as the memorial service began. Doug was unable to speak, I was not able to give the eulogy: I was very sick. Pat did the honors—he spoke of the wonderful times he had with Danny and tried to keep his emotions in check as he recalled one time at a comedy club. Danny was much more humorous than the man on stage. Pat's tribute left me smiling.

The chapel was completely full, and one by one I spoke to every person as they offered me their support. It was devastating, since just last year we were all so happy at our wedding. I was distant and barely cordial with Mother. I spent the rest of the day at home trying to rest. My mouth was swollen, my fever was raging, and I knew I would need my strength for the long drive tomorrow for the funeral. That night I still was having strange experiences, and I would drift in and out of sleep. My cat lay beside me all night—he too was acting very strange. He would wander around the house meowing, and he was very agitated. He knew that Danny was gone.

It was now time to start the most dreaded day of my life. I was shocked when I looked in the mirror and saw that all of my hair turned gray! I was horrified! The stress truly was too much for my body. I spoke to my very close friend Joan who was devastated for me, she was in Hawaii and felt terrible she could not be here with me, I love her very much, her voice was exactly what I needed to hear to give my spirit a lift. I phoned my other close friend Lynelle who was also out of town, I completely fell apart during our conversation. Cindy & Marie were with me for the two-and-a-half-hour drive to the small town where Danny was born. Tensions were very high when I arrived. His mother didn't speak to me, and his sister was very short. One detail that they failed to tell me was that the entire service was in Spanish. His daughter was sitting beside me and my heart was deeply saddened that she couldn't understand what was being said. The priest spoke for only a few moments in English and what he said enraged me, "While Danny was on his death bed, he finally allowed God to enter into his life. He saw the error of his ways and now he can have a proper burial and rest in peace." Connie was sitting behind me, and she was just as horrified as I was. Needless to say, I was ready for the day to end. After the ceremony, I didn't speak much to his family and quickly left town. I was shattered and filled with remorse. I felt like I had betrayed Danny's wishes. The only bright spot in the whole day was when I first arrived in town and went to the pond to feed the ducks and have a picnic lunch where Danny had always brought me.

As the days passed, the reality of being widowed was slowly sinking in. It was a twisted emotional experience—I hated being in our home alone, yet it was the only place I wanted to be. I was very sick and found myself being diagnosed with Chronic Fatigue Syndrome, pneumonia, and exhaustion. I was completely drained and would find myself needing bed rest for over three months.

All the arguing with family members sent my health into a downward spiral. I knew in my heart and soul that Danny was with me. I was beginning to realize I was in a no-win situation. On one hand, Danny had prepared me to be strong and to "get on with it," as he put it, and to not let the grief completely consume me, but rather to be drenched in the "cup of life." Sadly, on the other hand, I was being chastised, judged, and condemned.

I spent my time over the next couple months finalizing Danny's affairs while trying to carve out a new relationship as he planned for me was proving to be extremely difficult. I was still recovering from chronic fatigue and pneumonia, Life isn't a book you can stick on a shelf! You have to force yourself through the next chapter of your life or you will suffocate yourself with misery. I knew I had to embrace life or I too would die.

I returned to the cemetery before Thanksgiving. I stopped by to see Danny's Mother, I always want her to know how much I love her. His Mother is so funny and spirited I am thankful that we can get along so well after all that had happened. Driving into the cemetery was very sobering, I tried not to crumble as I approached his grave. I had designed the headstone for his grave. It was a large granite heart with an angel praying on one side and a left-handed golfer on the other. It was beautiful. I had overwhelming flashbacks of that chilly Christmas morning when Danny first brought me here.

I learned that Chronic Fatigue Syndrome greatly inhibited my daily functions. My friends were vital for helping me. I was completely drained of all of my energy, and it made regaining a normal daily routine impossible. I knew that facing the Holidays would be very difficult, new love doesn't replace the previous; nor did I expect it to, it does however allow you to live! I knew having a relationship would be odd to some people that were close to me. We had to create our own life together while concluding one that was completely on the other end of the spectrum. We had to accept that there would be extremely difficult and tumultuous days. It wasn't easy, my emotions were out of control! I felt undeserving, guilty, shameful, and I had lost respect for myself and it showed. It was a daily struggle trying not let myself be angry for having to start over again and fearful that I didn't have the strength to endure anymore hardship that may come. I didn't want to hurt anyone else; I felt that Danny and I had done enough damage. I did my best in spite of myself to forge this new relationship. I tried to focus on all of the blessings that God had given me, and I reminded myself daily that Life is far too precious to waste on trivial emotions and circumstances that I couldn't change to see me through the dark days! We did raise more than a few eyebrows as we became involved. Again the dynamic of our inner circle was changing; our friends did their best to be supportive. Our conversations had always been straight forward, especially regarding this issue.

All I wanted to do was concentrate on things that made me feel good. I donated Danny's wardrobe to a charity. With Christmas coming, I knew that his clothing would be able to help so many people who were in need and besides, they weren't doing any good hanging in the closest. I chose the charity Big Brothers & Big Sisters to give his things to. The organization does outstanding work helping young people who are struggling in their lives. I carefully folded every pair of pants and every shirt, remembering vividly every time he had worn them. I packed box after box; I kept a few things and gave some to his closest friends. I taped the boxes shut, drew a big red heart on each one with a red marker, and wrote "With love." Next, I contacted the doctor's office and asked if the patients could use Danny's supplies. Danny had accumulated quite an inventory, and I couldn't just throw them away when I knew that it could spare someone just one day of pain. It gave me a wonderful sense of peace knowing that I could help in that way. I gave mom some of Danny's things that would give her comfort and hopefully repair the distance, she was delighted and we had a wonderful time together, I let the rest go and we moved on.

Facing my first Christmas without Danny was extremely difficult even with a new relationship being forged. I was barely well enough to travel. I thought California was the perfect remedy that would help soothe my soul; spending time at the ocean immersed in the healing rays of the sun seemed ideal for my emotional and physical well-being. I was WRONG. I ended up being rushed to the hospital only a few days into my vacation. I was experiencing severe chest pains, I was gasping for air, and it hurt to breathe. doctors rushed me in for testing—they suspected I was having a heart attack. Merry Christmas. I had walking pneumonia, internal organ swelling, Chronic Fatigue Syndrome, and I was suffering from severe panic attacks. I was very ill and had to return home.

With another New Year beginning, I had to challenge myself to regain my life. I had such an enormous amount of sorrow and pain that I desperately wanted to embrace each day and laugh and smile again. I didn't want to be filled with sorrow and anger, it was a day-to-day struggle; I did not want my grief to shut me down or to hold me back but it was, it was like a steamroller destroying everything in its path. Grief can either destroy your life or inspire it. New love isn't the cure-all I expected it to be, we were two very different people. Memories aren't erasable or sometimes even changeable; a realization I was quickly learning.

After Danny made his transition, I kept in contact with his doctor and staff. You can't spend over one year of your life with them and not become close. When I visited the hospital, I would always stop by the floor where Danny and I spent so much of our married life together. The nurses were wonderful, caring individuals, and I loved seeing them, one in particular was Rose, she had a warm smile that brightened even our worst moments, she cared for Danny daily with love. Danny adored her. When I was well enough I would also spend time visiting with the people who were facing serious health issues and their families. We would share ideas, and I helped give them insight into difficult situations. Helping people was fast becoming my Mood Food. I knew exactly what their concerns were and the advice that could help them. I was able to give them comfort and reassurance, and most importantly, I listened with a compassionate, loving heart. I surprised even myself! If anyone had told me that I would enjoy the hospital, I would have told them that they were crazy! A special bond develops between people stricken with cancer that made me want to extend myself in every way possible, whether a brief phone call or a lengthy discussion. I soon found it very rewarding, rejuvenating, and uplifting.

Even as I tried to start a new life I knew the void and emptiness would not vanish so easily. It truly is a transition, you will never be that person you once were, nor will you ever look at life with the same innocence or stupidity again. You have to force yourself to move forward. It is bittersweet. You are grateful to God for giving you the courage and the strength to move on, but you never forget why you are having to.

As the months flew by, the emptiness and stinging pain were still present. The more I tried to force myself to move on with my life, the harder it became. I was plagued by illness, and having to spend month after month in bed made recovery seem a million miles away. My saving grace had always been ballet dancing, but that was clearly not possible. I had to practice meditation to soothe my spirit, and I would listen to jazz or classical music. Remembering every day that I shared these vital tools that brought such satisfaction to Danny also helped me to heal.

Facing the anniversary of Danny's transition was very painful. I knew that he was with me, guiding and coaching me. I could always feel his presence just like he told me, and I knew he was with me in my dreams as well. I did miss the sound of his voice and his laughter very much.

I found comfort in sharing time with my friends. I was learning that grief really is a process and just when you think you're recovering fairly well, you get consumed by tidal waves of emotion. I really was hoping that the second Holiday season would not be so difficult, but I was still plagued by Chronic Fatigue Syndrome and was full of anxiety. The strife between Mom and I was fading and I wanted to have a wonderful holiday season. Mom was singing in the Christmas program at the church. The production was spectacular, but I found myself in deep sorrow as I sat all by myself among the families who were so happy. The church was so beautifully decorated—the candles were glowing brightly; the music from the choir was wonderful, and there I sat with tears streaming down my face, quietly sobbing amid all of the festivities. I missed the bliss my life once had.

I decided to go to the cemetery. I decorated a tiny tree I had bought, and I covered his grave with poinsettias and placed two large white prayer candles next to the card I had picked out for him. The air was very chilly and crisp with the smell of pine. The little lights on the tree were twinkling in the night, and the glow from the candles illuminated the headstone. I felt an enormous sense of peace wash over me as I sat beside the candles. I said a Christmas prayer for him, and I promised not to let the past hinder my future, to always know that in my heart, soul, and mind he was in heaven and I didn't need to feel such anger and deep sorrow. As I was leaving his grave a hush swept through the air, and when the wind stopped blowing there was silence...

With this New Year beginning, regaining a normal daily routine was difficult. As the weeks quickly turned into months, I was still plagued with Chronic Fatigue Syndrome. It left me exhausted. I spent much of my time on the phone offering support to those in need. I quickly learned that the best way to help yourself is by helping others. It seemed that everyone who was entering my life either had cancer or knew someone who did. I often spoke to Vicki our nurse, and she told me that her patients were greatly benefiting from her massage therapy, and that she discovered a healing gift in her hands that allowed her patients tremendous relief. She encouraged my work with those in need, and I knew that I was finding my true purpose and destiny.

Even when the path you are on is full of potholes, if you give of yourself with a loving, passionate spirit, you will find your greatest gift is your perseverance and belief in yourself no matter how rocky the road becomes.

I returned to Danny's grave on our wedding anniversary and left flowers, candles, and a card. It was a very special day for me, and it always will be. The emptiness was slowly dissipating, and I knew that I had to be patient with myself and never stop striving for the life I wanted. I had to force myself not to let it kill my spirit as well as anymore relationships. I focused on others in need to see me through.

The Holiday season was here once again, and I was facing my third Christmas as a widow. I did not find myself in such deep sorrow or feeling alone. I had come so far, I truly had many reasons to be joyous and festive. I was still recovering from my illness, and I just accepted the fact that it would take a great deal of time and I had to be patient. When I was feeling well, I indulged in my passion for dancing. I was finding a whole new world of friends and meeting people who wanted and needed my guidance. That left my spirit rejuvenated. God truly has angels here on earth. I see them daily.

Murphy's Law decided to rear its ugly head again, and over the course of the next several years I found myself in and out of the hospital needing extensive care and therapy. I was forced to be on a barrage of medications, herbs, and supplements. They had a tremendous impact on my overall well-being. The side effects of some of them were so hellacious; gee, do I want a heart attack today, stroke, or blood clots? I'll keep the illness that I have, thank you very much! I tried to stick to an herbal healing RX as much as possible. It was during that extensive recovery period that I had a clear direction of how I wanted to move forward with my life. I committed myself to working with people who were facing a serious diagnosis, specializing in Hospice care. It is why God made me. I started holding support groups for families and friends who needed direction. I gave them alternatives to handle the challenges they had encountered in their lives along with a huge dose of compassion and love. I quickly saw smiles and a new-found sense of hope on the faces of the people that I was speaking to. Each time I phoned or saw them, they were at a point where they were about to give up, and I was able to give them the focus that they needed. It was also during my recovery that I started writing this book. I am very happy to say that Danny's family is doing well. I talk to them frequently and see them when I visit Danny's grave.

As the years have tumbled by, I have tried to use faith and strength as my guide. My lack of patience and anger were slow to ease. Meditation, dancing, and music have nurtured my spirit. They say that time heals all wounds, but I know that it is what you do with your time that allows you to heal. Moving forward is not easy, and I have stumbled many times in my quest for happiness. My resolve and passion are undaunted. Unfulfilled desires can keep you from moving forward. Self respect and integrity can be difficult to re-gain once it's been given away. I never forget about the past, because it keeps me humble, thankful, grounded, and relatable. I am also reminded daily of how far I have come and how much further I have to go, and that there is a passionate new life ahead. I never gave up or let my fears hold me back.

As I write these last pages, I never imagined myself giving support groups, seminars, or being able to help so many sensational organizations, and I certainly had no intention of writing this guidebook until I saw the demand for it. I see God's grace, mercy, and forgiveness everyday, working intently in my life. Carving out a new life and destiny has not been an easy journey—if it were it wouldn't mean a darn thing. Through our tragedies come our greatest triumphs. I feel sensational when I can make a positive impact in someone's life through my own experiences. My life has a new direction with the same burning passion that fueled my love and compassion for Danny. Love is an extremely powerful force coupled with a desire to make a positive difference in people's lives. I have found that the stinging emptiness that would grip my soul is vanishing. I was finding out that grief is a slow process with many junctures and dips. When I was able to better I did. For as much as I have shared with you there are many conversations, circumstances, and situations that will never be written about. Loyalty, love, and privacy are paramount in my life and in the lives of those around me. It is expected-received-given- unconditionally—Unwritten. It is by that in which character is re-defined, formed. Justified by grace, self-respect and integrity restored!

I want you to use this story as a tool, learn from my advice, mistakes, and shortcomings, and practice what you read. Take action in your life, it is far too precious to waste on things that don't truly matter. You must surround yourself with love for yourself. It is vital to your emotional and physical well-being. Never give up! Love, respect, and friendship will see you through your darkest hour. Remember there is always someone who needs your love and care, someone is suffering much more than you. You too can be the answer to someone's prayers, the question is, are you listening? God will light your path if you let him! Move forward with your life and be at peace with yourself and find peace in those around you. If I can do it after all that I have endured in my short life, so can you—remember it is a daily process. Get rid of anger, resentment, guilt, shame, and condemnation! Do everything in your power to keep your faith intact! Life truly is a treasure chest.

The Beginning?

NOTIONS & POTIONS

The following pages are designed to help you be more prepared for the journey ahead.

Start a notebook for your insurance and hospital paperwork. BE ORGANIZED! It will save you time and energy.

Make copies of all documents being sent to Social Security and your company benefits department, just in case of lost mail.

Make a list for contact names. Try to deal with the same people at your insurance company, Social Security, and the hospital. It is a good idea to keep in touch with these organizations on a regular basis to make sure that you are informed. No one likes unexpected surprises, i.e., benefit deadlines and phone appointments as well as medication dosage.

Always take a pad of paper and pen with you to EVERY doctor's appointment and tests. Write down any questions you have and the answer that is given. Your mind is racing in many directions; it is very easy to misunderstand what was said.

Learn about your treatments, diagnosis and medications. Find out what your body will be ingesting and how to deal with side effects.

Arm yourself with information about your illness, you are a Soldier going to war against your disease so be prepared!

Ask to see every test result, x-rays and scans that have been performed. This will give you a greater understanding of your health.

Put small message boards on your refrigerator and in the bathroom and write down every time you take your medication and what foods you need to eat before hand.

WARNING: Be aware of any increased medication and mood-swings. Are you taking too much of a prescription for pain? You may need to make an adjustment, ask your pharmacist and alert your doctor. What worked for you in the beginning may not be as effective any longer. INVESTIGATE!

Be aware that your appetite will fluctuate, add new things to your diet. Keep finger foods on hand. A whole piece of fruit or sandwich may look overwhelming, but when cut into bite size pieces it can be a creative way to enhance your diet. You must eat!

My husband hated drinking Ensure, even the sight of the cans would make him angry. I would make him milkshakes with fresh strawberries and Ice cream along with Ensure, and I would hide the cans. Out of sight, out of mind. He loved them. Be creative!

A peppermint lotion foot massage is an excellent remedy for tension and fatigue.

Chamomile herbal tea is excellent for relaxation and can help relieve mouth sores from chemotherapy.

When you're having a difficult day try relaxing with soothing music. Jazz, classical, or even nature soundtracks are my favorite picks.

Start and finish each day with meditation. Visualize yourself in a serene environment, the beach is perfect. Picture yourself healthy, vital, and strong. This will allow you to start and finish each day focused with a calm sense of inner self.

Poetry is the perfect way to share time with the one you love.

Laughter truly is the best medicine, spend at least one or two hours a day watching funny movies or even cartoons. Danny loved Whoopi Goldberg and the Looney Tunes characters to boost his mood.

Keep your atmosphere bright and cheery with plants and music. You must make an effort to keep yourself energized and in good spirits.

Play games! Do not dwell on your illness. Scrabble, Monopoly, and Battleship are great distractions. Travel sizes are perfect.

Lavender oil is excellent for an aromatherapy massage. It will soothe your soul.

Apricot and Vanilla scented candles help provide the perfect atmosphere for meditation and massage.

I found that drinking protein shakes mixed with apple juice, wheat germ oil, and bananas gives my body the nutrients I craves, find out what works for you. (yes, it's yummy too!)

Prayer works! Pray often, read the Bible daily, it will give you great comfort. God never gives us more to handle than we are able to. I have included a few fantastic, healing scriptures in the Resource Guide.

Find out what support groups your hospital offers. Sharing stories with other patients can be very helpful!

Hospice is a wonderful organization. Make the call when you are in need of help.

Read inspirational books and stories, you can create your own hope. *Love, Medicine & Miracles*, and the *Chicken Soup for the Soul* series are a fantastic place to start. Empower your spirit.

Music has been proven to boost your immune system. USE IT!
Natural herbs can enhance your health and well-being. If you aren't familiar with them, make certain you consult a professional for complete information.

WARNING: DO NOT LET YOURSELF FALL VICTIM TO UNPROVEN TREATMENTS! Do not let your condition allow your judgment to become clouded. Unfortunately you become an easy target for QUACKS. Listen to your heart, and be very leery about treatments promising amazing results. Do not play Russian Roulette with your life. Find reputable Doctors whose focus isn't money.

Additional oils and teas that can enhance your spirit:
Rosemary and Juniper are excellent for mental and physical stimulation. Ylang Ylang and Sandalwood are wonderful for meditation and relaxation. Geranium is also ideal for relaxation.

RESOURCE GUIDE

The very best way to fight cancer is to arm yourself with information; at the time of Danny's illness, information was very hard to come by. These are just a few that I put together to narrow your search and help you on your journey.

Cancer Web Sites:

Cancer Research Foundation of America
This Foundation deals with the following cancers: Lung, breast, prostate, skin, colorectal, and cervical. Prevention through scientific research and education.
http://www.cancerprevention.org

Cancer Organization Institute
This Organization provides clinical trials, reviews and information to medical professionals as well as the general public.
http://www.cancergroup.com

This Close for Cancer Research, Inc
Providing cancer research through charity events, leukemia, care and support groups.
http://www.thisclose.org

Sidney Kimmel Cancer Center
This research center is independent and non-profit committed to cancer and related diseases through biological therapies.
http://www.skcc.org

American Cancer Society
This outstanding organization is committed to helping everyone who is facing cancer! Research, treatment and patient services are able to provide a complete strategy.
http://www.cancer.org

HopeLink
Provides information and patient services regarding clinical trials, new drug and medical developments.
http://www.hopelink.com

T.J. Martell Foundation
This Foundation specializes in aids, leukemia, and cancer research.
http://www.tjmartellfoundation.org

American Society of Clinical Oncology
This clinical organization is the leading cancer information center for not only Oncologists and medical specialists but patients as well. Their Web site is a necessity for those facing cancer.
http://www.asco.org

HEALING BIBLE SCRIPTURES

The Bible has countless scriptures that can give you comfort, strength, and vital healing tools. The Number One daily priority is to pray diligently. Get angry at the disease, not God. He is not some mystical unreachable creation. Don't let religion get in the way of your healing and wellness.

Forgiveness through mercy and grace are the essential keys. I wish and regret not using or having this wisdom and spiritual foundation. Let it be a blessing for your life!

II Corinthians 1:20
For no matter how many promises God has made, they are "yes"
In Christ.

II Corinthians 10:4
The weapons we fight with are not the weapons of the world. On the contrary, they have divine power to abolish strongholds.

Philippians 2:13
For it is God who works in you and will act according to his good purpose.

Romans 8:11
And if the Spirit who raised Jesus from the dead is living in you, he who raised Christ from the dead will also give life to your mortal bodies through his Spirit, who lives in you.

James 4:10
Humble yourself before the Lord, and he will lift you up.

James 5:13-15
Is any one of you in trouble? He should pray. Is anyone happy? Let him sing songs of praise. Is any one of you sick? He should call the elders of the church to pray over him and anoint his head with oil in the name of the Lord. And the prayer offered in faith will make the sick person well; the Lord will raise him up. If he has sinned, he will be forgiven.

1 Peter 2:24
He himself bore our sins in his body on the tree, so that we might die to sins and live for righteousness; by his wounds you have been healed.

Deuteronomy 7:15
The Lord will keep you from every disease. He will not inflict on you the horrible diseases you knew in Egypt, but he will inflict them on all who hate you.

Psalm 41:3-4
The Lord will sustain him on his sickbed and restore him from his bed of illness. For he said, "O Lord, have mercy on me; heal me, for I have sinned against you."

Source: *NIV Rainbow Study Bible*

In Loving Memory for my friend

MARIE E. SCHWARTZ

My soul aches for you and my spirit lifts you up daily. May God bless you in Heaven for your passionate unwavering Activism and your tireless work to END the Canadian Seal Hunt! Your friends worldwide at the Humane Society continue your legacy of love and passion for these precious animals. May your motto live on and inspire us all. Your friends miss you dearly.

CLUB SANDWICHES NOT SEALS
End the Canadian seal hunt now

www.ingramcontent.com/pod-product-compliance
Ingram Content Group UK Ltd.
Pitfield, Milton Keynes, MK11 3LW, UK
UKHW051137260726
13967UKWH00010B/3109

9 781419 657443